Praise for *The Road to Credit Repair*

You will find thousands of credit repair books for sale today, each claiming to raise your credit scores instantly. However, you won't find a narrated, factual accounting, of how a million dollars in debt was overcome in ten months by real people as you will with *The Road to Credit Repair*. With the inspiration and compassion of a true champion, Deborah M. Dennis imparts her personal experience of falling over a million dollars into debt as she discloses the strategy she innovated for victory.

With a mission to help someone else side-step the pitfalls and predatory practices that can be associated with the credit repair business, *The Road to Credit Repair* could not appear on the scene at a more timely moment. With credit scores caught in a downward spiral as a consequence of the foreclosure rate and an ailing economy, this book is an honest self-help for repairing your credit and reducing debt. It is paramount for anyone desiring to alleviate debt, improve their credit score, and commence building wealth.

I first met Deborah at a luncheon where I was raising money for one of my charities. In our very first conversation, I could see the genuineness in her desire to tell her story. She walked up to me, asked for my autograph, and we engaged in conversation as though we had known each other a lifetime. Later she became my protégé as she embarked upon writing her first book.

I can remember when I wrote my first book, *The Christmas Box*. It was for someone else, my daughters—a gift at Christmas. Deborah and I have something in common here as we each wrote our first book with the mindset of giving someone else a gift. *The Road to Credit Repair* is her gift to all who are in need of assistance with repairing their credit and reducing their debt. It is also a must have for anyone who wants to learn how to generate income as they sleep—residual income—to supplement their finances during retirement.

As she shares her story of how she fell into debt, her bright, effervescent personality is personified in her writing. I can only think that it takes a mighty special person to confront adversity and protect the dreams of someone else as she did for her homebuyers. Hers is an amazing story of triumph over adversity, and while she implemented strategies to ameliorate her own predicament, she kept a watchful eye on the well being of her homebuyers—because as she says, "It was the right thing to do."

It gives me honor and a sense of pride to have a protégé produce a book of the quality of *The Road to Credit Repair*. With this book, she restores hope and invigorates a desire to achieve financial independence through multiple streams of income. Her innovative blueprint for reducing debt, coupled with common sense budgeting, will absolutely set you on track for amassing wealth quickly. She will be there in mind and spirit to help you each step of the way.

- RICHARD PAUL EVANS
#1 New York Times bestselling author of *The Christmas Box*

THE ROAD TO
CREDIT REPAIR

THE ROAD TO
CREDIT REPAIR

Improve Your Credit Score and
Turn YOUR DEBT into a POSITIVE NET

DEBORAH M. DENNIS

BookWise publishing

The Road to Credit Repair
Improve Your Credit Score and Turn Your Debt Into a Positive Net
Deborah M. Dennis

Published by BookWise Publishing
65 E. Wadsworth Park Drive, Suite 110, Draper, UT 84020
www.bookwise.com

For quantity discounts call 972 293-7727
Visit our Web site at www.theroadtocreditrepair.com

Book design: Eden Design, Salt Lake City, Utah

Library of Congress Cataloging-in-Publication Data
Dennis, Deborah M.
The Road to Credit Repair: Improve Your Credit Score and
Turn Your Debt Into a Positive Net / Deborah M. Dennis

ISBN: 13-978-0-9796689-0-6
10 9 8 7 6 5 4 3 2 1
First Printing

PRINTED IN THE UNITED STATES OF AMERICA

This book is dedicated to my grandparents, Mama Bet and Papa, and my surrogate fathers, John and T-bo, with loving memory.

To my husband, W. T., for your presence in my past and my now, and for all that we aspire to become tomorrow.

To my children, Nikisha and Chevella "Joy," and my grands, Kynidi and Frederick, for having shown me what the future beholds.

And to my Mom, Thyra, for being the root of my inspiration.

TABLE OF CONTENTS

FOREWORD

I have been watching Deborah Dennis grow her real estate career since 2006. As a member of my Inner Wealth Training class, she expounded her million dollars in net assets by working to improve her inner wealth, using my training to understand the six major components that make us whole: mind, body, being, money, people, and time.

Over the past year, it has been interesting and quite amazing at times to see what she and her husband have accomplished despite many obstacles. Your average entrepreneur would have thrown in the towel long ago, but every time defeat has reared its ugly head, they've managed to fight back. The word "awesome" will come to mind as you read about how they fought to overcome adversity and sustain their dream of being entrepreneurs in the real estate industry.

You will enjoy reading this book and if you take away with you even half of what Deborah is trying to teach, you will be far ahead of the average American who is buried in debt. Not only will you learn how to improve your credit score and stay out of debt for good, but you will also find ways to invest in your future. Owning your own home is the very best way to invest—not to mention all the wonderful ways owning real estate can add value to your personal wealth.

Deborah exhibits enlightened wealth. I admire Deborah for giving back to her community and for her efforts to enhance academic opportunities in the economically depressed areas of her city. Throughout the numerous ups and downs in her life, she has taken the time to help someone in need, do volunteer work, and teach real estate investing and leveraging techniques to inspire others to seriously consider building nest eggs through real estate investing. How many of us reach the top of our careers without a thought to help someone else attain what we have? Deb looks after the "little guy" every day and I urge you to take advantage of all that she knows.

From whom would you rather take advice: a professor with all kinds of degrees in finance who never got around to buying a house, a financial planner or investment banker who has never been unable to pay his bills each month, or someone who has faced financial ruin and exhibited the tenacity to overcome it all to create a million net? Deb, of course, is the latter. She experienced a very comfortable lifestyle, took big risks, became buried in debt, fought her way out of debt using all of the consumer protection laws to her advantage, and made some very smart investments. Wouldn't you rather learn from someone like her?

This is the key message to take away from this book: Even while bill collectors are knocking on your door, never be afraid to start that new venture and create a viable plan to promote success, invest in real estate, or enact decisions that will increase your wealth and ensure your future financial security. Use her experiences to shore up your confidence.

So get ready to step onto the road to credit repair and improve your credit score so that you can turn your debt into a positive net. Deb will change the way you think about the struggle to eliminate your debt. Using her IPO strategy, you will learn to courageously describe your financial situation in writing, to see your status clearly, and to formulate a plan to improve your financial circumstances in a simple, tabular design on paper.

I have confidence that you can do it. I encourage you to do it. Follow Deborah's lead for the successful reduction of your debt, which will improve your credit score. Then with your improved credit score, start concentrating on establishing your money tree. You can do it because you are an awesome individual.

- **ROBERT G. ALLEN**
#1 Bestselling Author of *Nothing Down*

Preface

What we are today is the result of our own past actions.
Whatever we wish to be in the future depends on our present actions.
Decide how you have to act now.
We are responsible for what we are, whatever we wish ourselves to be.
We have the power to make ourselves.

— PRAVS J.

This book is a true, real-life story of how my husband and I eliminated more than $1.325 million dollars of debt in less than ten months. How did we acquire this much debt? Having worked in a private industry as a software engineer for fifteen years, I was tired of being "tired of." I wanted to spend more time with my kids and have a more flexible schedule. So I quit my job cold turkey on the morning of May 12, 1992 and I walked out unemployed and unhappy, not knowing where to go or what to do next. All I knew was that I was tired and fed up, and I never wanted to work as an employee ever again. I never wanted anyone else to have the kind of control over my life that came with a nine to five. Whatever it took, I was willing to do it and would do it to keep it that way.

At the time, our credit scores were decent— between 620 and 650. My husband was making it as a self-employed residential general contractor. We decided to join forces and make a go out of a business in the construction market. This was the beginning of the story—a long story of hardship and struggles and triumph over adversity.

Times were hard then in the construction industry and the debt from money borrowed to do deals just kept growing, growing, and growing. Before we knew it, we were in debt with everyone—the IRS, vendors, family, friends, credit card companies, etc. No end was in sight. To make a long story short, our incredible debt started when we sold our home, borrowed a million dollars from a hard money lender at a whopping eighteen percent interest, and commenced building a housing development.

Shortly after, the housing market became depressed in Texas, so things quickly went awry, especially after 9/11. The money from the sale of the house was spent and the hard-money lender held title to our land, grasping it tightly to play us like puppets on a string.

Eventually, he used that title in an attempt to steal our land and our dreams. He stopped the construction funds from flowing, which momentarily prohibited our progress and left us vulnerable to failure. At the point at which he finally cut the funding, we were unprepared. We had four houses underway with no plan, no money, and no hope for completing or fulfilling what we had started. His calculated move left us powerless to complete construction on four custom homes. Without any means and resources to finish them, we had fallen upon sinking sand. All we had left was the debt—his and all the others before him and after him. We were about to lose everything.

How did we survive? We stepped forward with faith and figured out how to use our real estate to our advantage. Our original plan included the building of three custom homes at less than fifty percent loan to value (LTV). These were still in our possession and they became our bank. Because the LTV was so good, in spite of our lack of creditworthiness, we were able to leverage these homes and mortgage them to pay off the debt and get the money to complete the construction. Then we sold the mortgages to eliminate the debt.

You must know that because I am writing this book, we triumphed over adversity. Afterwards, I went to work on our credit scores and, fortunately, was able to raise them above 700. Within one year's time, our net worth surpassed one million dollars. The entire ordeal transformed my cavalier attitude toward money, credit, and debt management into that of a serious wealth builder.

This synoptic accounting of a large amount of debt turned into a million net does not begin to capture the poignancy and implausibility of the full story. I disclose every detail of how we persevered to overcome trouble, disaster, hardship, and pain in my book *In God We Trust: The Mindset of a Successful Real Estate Investor*. I invite you to pick up a copy when it hits the shelves during the summer of 2008 and I hope it will inspire you to never give up on your dreams.

Your story may be different, but the end result can be the same. Yesterday, perhaps, you were coasting. You had your "head above water," were "making ends meet," "getting by," "juggling finances," and once in a while, "giving in" and buying that expensive gadget you really couldn't afford. You were "hoping" that a better job, or lottery winnings, or "something," would erase your money worries. Somehow, though, in spite of the obstacles and the juggling of the debt, you still felt that you were "coming out okay."

You rarely missed a credit card payment and if you did, you doubled up the next month, even if it was just a little late. Bill collectors were not knocking on your door and you had enough food to put on the table. You believed that if you could just "tighten your belt," you could pay off your debts and maybe even buy a house. However, your wake-up call came when you tried to buy a new car or apply for a mortgage and found out your credit report was a mess. Your score was low from all of those late payments and too much other debt—unbalanced debt, which has caused you to not even be close to qualifying for a loan.

That was the something that happened to cause your light to come on: "You're not doing okay!" So you bought this book because you want to do better. You want to win at debt reduction. You want to build wealth. Trust me! It is not over yet!

Yet!

Why "yet?"

I say, "Not over yet" *because there is hope.*

I have three main goals for this book. The first is to educate you. You will know just about everything there is to know about credit repair and debt elimination by the time I expose you to my successes, as I lead you down the road to credit repair. You will learn strategies that will enable and inspire you as you pay down your debt, increase your credit score, change your spending habits, and transform your cavalier thinking about debt into a more positive, goal-oriented attitude that will motivate you to build wealth.

In helping you to build your wealth, we will address everything from acquiring an understanding of credit, debt, bankruptcy, and identity theft to how to handle bill collectors and when to seek support from a credit-counseling service. In short, you will come to know your options and how to execute them. Through the use of spreadsheets and real case studies, you will be exposed to using systematic methods for reducing debt and improving your credit score. You will become a walking expert on debt-reducing techniques and using credit to your advantage while you accumulate a positive net through real estate investing.

The second goal is to empower you. You will know how to find the resources, employ knowledge, and acquire the right attitude to change your current situation—to lay a great foundation for the future. Your days of being victimized because of past behavior are about to end. Through this book, you will be able to step forward with the know-how to make use of the laws and programs designed to help you to restore your good credit. Once you learn how the system works, you'll have the confidence to make it work for *YOU*.

The third goal is to inspire you. Perhaps you think that your only option is to file for bankruptcy protection or just to pack up and leave town. Trust me, you do have other options. If we can dig ourselves out of a million dollars in debt, you can dig yourself out of yours. All you need is some faith, determination, perseverance, and action.

So read on and be prepared to change your life by repairing the past and stepping forward in search of a brilliant future. I will be right there beside you…*every step of the way.*

CHAPTER 1

Credit: The Good Side and the Bad

Credit is not income. It is not a right,
nor is it something bestowed upon everyone.
It is yours to use as long as it's not abused.
It equates to money—someone else's—that's shared at a price.
Credit can be your best friend—but with too much,
it will become your worst enemy.

—DEBORAH M. DENNIS

I hate to see bad credit stifle the dreams of those who want to do better—people who have the good intentions to pay back debt, but who just cannot make it happen because of circumstances beyond their control. Perhaps it started when you married an uncontrolled spender who arrived with $100,000 in student loans and other debts that were not revealed while you were dating. Or you and your spouse were living paycheck to paycheck when a medical crisis hit, forcing you to live on one income with thousands of dollars of hospital bills to pay. Downsizing! Mortgage rates adjusting! A fire! The economy! Maybe you are a person who lacks the discipline and structure to pay your bills on time, but you have the money. You are just sloppy when it comes to your creditworthiness. Worse yet, maybe you were a victim of identity theft and, because of someone else, you now have the nightmare of cleaning up your credit history. Whatever the reason, you have a job to do and the task ahead of you seems too hard to tackle. Don't despair! Have faith!

> *If you think you can win, you can win. Faith is necessary to victory.*
> — WILLIAM HAZLITT

Because I have successfully gone through what you are now going through, I can identify with your situation. Therefore, I have the experience to help you. It wasn't until I hit rock bottom that I realized I needed to take control of my finances and understand my credit score—and all the consequences of a bad one. Otherwise, I would have forever been saddled with the stigma of what bad credit would buy: NOTHING!

Feel good about yourself! You took the first big step toward restoring your financial health when you bought this book. If you gain an understanding of the purpose of credit and follow my advice step by step, you will be well on your way to repairing the past and building your future. I know that you want to do it. Please know that I am here to help you reach the journey's end.

I feel that in this first chapter it is extremely important to give you a brief overview of credit and how we can use it to improve our daily lives. Throughout my career, I was exposed to the importance of creditworthiness and its value as the key to building my business, gaining assets and amassing wealth. I had to embrace the concept and develop a personal understanding of how it works. I had to transform, literally, my way of thinking.

But before we delve into the tactics of using credit in a positive way, I will give you several pointers that can help you identify when credit is your friend and when it's just being downright nasty. With an intimate understanding of credit—what it is as well as its true purpose—you will be well prepared for the wealth of information to follow. The first thing that I want you to become intimately familiar with is this:

In order to be granted credit and borrow at the best rates, you must gain an understanding of credit-reporting procedures and how debt affects credit scoring. However, it is not enough just to be educated about creditworthiness. To stay creditworthy, wisdom has to be coupled with making good choices in establishing debt.

What Is Credit?

Technically speaking, credit is money granted by an institution—such as a bank or credit-granting institution—based on your ability to pay the money back, usually with additional interest. I like to view credit as renting money because it has to be given back, and given back with interest. Of course, credit can also be granted by a friend, relative, or private investor.

We usually pay for the privilege of credit. Unless you are one of those who pay your credit cards in full each month, you will be paying an additional amount of money in interest. This extra fee covers the risk of loaning money to you, *and* it makes a profit for the lender.

This is where many of us get into trouble. For example, let's say you have to have that huge, flat-screen TV that everyone else seems to own, at a cost of $2,000. If the interest rate is seventeen percent on the credit card you use and it takes you five years to pay it off, you will have spent nearly $3,000! This example uses seventeen percent simple interest on an installment loan with a monthly payment of $49. Let's calculate charging this debt to a credit card at twenty-nine percent interest. At this rate, you will have paid over $4,500 for the television—more than double the price. Now that's a lesson learned the hard way: *Always* pay attention not just to what you're purchasing, but also to how much it will cost you in the long run to purchase it. My philosophy: "Do the math" before you buy!

There Is a Good Side...

Some days, when we are buried in debt, it is hard to remember that there is a positive side to using credit. First of all, it buys us time. If we need to make a purchase today—say, at the grocery store—but we don't get paid for another two weeks, we can whip out that credit card and pay the money back later.

The best example of using credit to our advantage is when we take out a loan to buy a house or investment property. Not only does a house provide a permanent shelter for you and your family, but if you buy in the right neighborhood, the house will appreciate in value. In addition, the mortgage interest you pay to the bank is tax deductible both as a homeowner and as an investor (if the investment becomes rental property).

This is an important point because we all have to pay to stay somewhere. We may as well pay to stay where the money invested can manifest as both a tax benefit and equity. If we buy investment properties on credit, in addition to the tax benefits, someone else can pay the loan off as long as the property is rented. This is smart debt—good debt. See? Credit is not all bad—you just have to know when it can be an advantage!

CREDIT	
Best Friend	*Worst Enemy*
Good Debt	**Bad Debt**
Assets—real estate, business	Clothes, stuff
Makes money	No value
Leads to good credit	Leads to ruin

A good credit history gives you choices. Coupled with the appropriate income, it can help you pass the credit test for the house for which you qualify or for the apartment you can afford; buy a reliable car; and borrow money to send your kids to college. With bad credit, on the other hand, your choices become extremely limited and usually result in a much lower standard of living. Added to this, if credit is granted to one with a low credit score and a poor credit history, chances are it will be granted with an exorbitant rate of interest.

The Down Side

There are some serious down sides and consequences of handling credit inappropriately. For one, if you cannot pay back the money you borrow on a credit card within thirty days, you will be paying a lot more for the items you charged—remember that flat-screen TV? In addition, if you take out too many loans and put too many purchases on credit cards, there is a real risk you won't be able to pay them all back on time. This is what wrecks your credit score —but we'll get into that in more detail later.

Sure, for a while, you can keep your head above water and make all those minimum payments, but it only takes one crisis—such as replacement of a major appliance, a major car repair, or an illness—to throw you off track. Let's not leave out temptation to do something other than spend the money paying bills—such as purchasing a new outfit, taking a trip, or impressing a friend with a night out on the town.

The fact is, overwhelming debt overwhelms, causing marital problems, illness, and a bad attitude. Overwhelming debt suffocates and it enslaves. You have to make your relationship with credit a delicate balancing act and borrow only what you can pay back within a short period of time. Exceptions include a long-term investment such as buying a house, which brings value into your life in many, many ways, or a car, when it becomes an absolute necessity.

Before we proceed any further, let's take a look at the three types of credit needed in order to establish a good credit history and increase a credit score.

Three Kinds of Credit

There are three kinds of credit that you should know about. If you take out a loan in any of these categories and pay it back on time, you will begin the journey of establishing a great credit history. In other words, to have good credit, you must first *use* credit.

A balanced credit report should have at least three open lines reporting in one of these areas: revolving, installment, and real estate. If you are starting out on the road to credit repair, you need to know where to step.

TYPES OF CREDIT NEEDED TO ESTABLISH A GOOD CREDIT SCORE

Type	Definition	Purchases	Structure	Value
Revolving	Repeatedly available up to a specified amount	Department store credit	Unsecured	No value
Installment loans	Repaid with a fixed number of equal payments	Car or furniture loan	Secured	Depreciates
Real estate	Mortgage loan paid over fifteen to thirty years	Home or rental property	Secured	Appreciates

Revolving credit gives you access to a specific amount of money that you can spend in any way you want—known as a "line of credit." For example, the bank will approve a loan of $1,000. You can either leave this money in the bank, use a little at a time, or spend it all at once. Another example of this kind of credit is a credit card—major or department store. You use the credit, and it replenishes as the debt is paid down. As you pay the money back, the lender collects interest on the amount used. These purchases normally have no value, and are often referred to as "empty" purchases.

An installment credit or loan grants you an amount of money that you receive immediately and then pay off with regular, fixed payments over a period of time. This includes embedded interest. An example of this type of loan is borrowing money to buy a car, business equipment, or furniture. The loan is secured by the purchase. The purchase is considered an asset in some cases, but the asset depreciates in value.

Real estate or mortgage loans relate to purchasing an item such as a house, home improvements, or investment property. These loans are normally amortized over ten, fifteen, twenty, or thirty years. Amortization is the process of repaying money, which was borrowed to purchase a home or other real estate, through regular monthly payments that include both principal and interest calculated over a specific period of time.

An amortization schedule can be referenced to get a complete snapshot of a mortgage repayment, and it is especially useful when trying to determine how much interest has been paid and what the current principal balance is. For an example of an amortization schedule, visit my website, www.theroadtocreditrepair.com. I provide the ability for you to create your own amortization schedule for either an existing or proposed mortgage.

There is one important distinction to note about these three kinds of credit. With revolving or installment credit, the debt you are incurring depreciates in most cases because the purchase may not always be an asset. You're actually borrowing money and repaying it with interest only to the benefit of the lender, when buying items such as clothing, furniture, toys, etc. which do not appreciate in value. I call this "bad debt!"

Exceptions to this theory are a car purchase used for work or business and business equipment. Even though these debts depreciate in value, they can be used to generate income. An installment loan for these types of purchases is a necessity and is unavoidable for most people; however, a car purchased unnecessarily is considered a bad debt.

In the case of a mortgage, you are purchasing or investing in property that will appreciate, or increase in value. I refer to this as "good debt" because it builds wealth. Though you repay the mortgage with interest, that interest is tax deductible. If the mortgage is for an investment, in addition to the tax benefits, the property can be an income producer. The thing to remember is this: I'd like to see you, over time, position yourself so that you only borrow money to build wealth. The best debt you can have is debt that appreciates, but first things first.

Credit Myths and Misinformation

You know what a myth is. I personally define it as something that is believed to be true, but is actually not true, and the belief is used to justify a specific position on an issue. There are far too many myths about credit to list in this book, but these are the ones I hear the most, and the ones that I want you to know the truth about:

Thirteen Common Myths and Misunderstandings About Credit

1. My bad credit will stay with me forever.

2. It doesn't matter how high the balances are on my credit cards as long as I make my minimum payments on time.

3. If I cosign a loan for a friend, it won't show up on my credit report or affect my credit.

4. If I am using credit responsibly and never get turned down for a loan, I have no need to request a copy of my credit report.

5. Once I pay an overdue bill or court judgment, or bring current any other missed payments, they will be removed from my credit report.

6. My divorce decree will take precedence over a credit obligation.

7. Lenders will only look at my credit score when deciding whether or not to loan me money.

8. My credit score will improve if I close out all my old cards that I don't really use any more.

9. I know poor credit will affect me financially, but it won't be an issue in any other part of my life.

10. If I get in over my head with credit, I can always file for bankruptcy protection.

11. It is okay to go over your credit limit if the store accepts it. That must mean that the credit card company authorized the purchase.

12. I should just avoid using credit cards all together.

13. My credit is so bad now, it will be destroyed forever.

Myth: My bad credit will stay with me forever.

Fact: The good news is that by law, negative information can only stay on your credit report for seven years and bankruptcies for ten. The most recent two years are the most important, as older information will hurt your credit score less.

Myth: It doesn't matter how high the balances are on my credit cards as long as I make my minimum payments on time.

Fact: It matters a lot how full your credit cards are, even if you make all minimum payments. Experts recommend only using thirty to forty percent of the available balance for each card, or it will show up as a negative on your credit report. To be safe, if I were to carry a balance, I would never spend over thirty-five percent of the credit limit.

Myth: If I cosign a loan for a friend, it won't show up on my credit report or affect my credit.

Fact: Cosigned loans do appear in your credit file. Not only are you held responsible for the repayment of the loan, it will definitely affect your credit history if it is not repaid on time. My advice is this: If you cosign a loan, micromanage the repayment of the loan. Your good credit is at stake.

Myth: If I am using credit responsibly and never get turned down for a loan, I have no need to request a copy of my credit report.

Fact: Studies have shown as much as eighty percent of people's credit reports contain mistakes, and up to one-third of these are big enough to be denied credit. It is important to review your credit report at least once per year. It is not necessary to purchase credit monitoring from the credit agencies. If you are at risk for identity theft, check your file every quarter.

Myth: Once I pay an overdue bill or court judgment, or take care of any other missed payments, they will be removed from my credit report.

Fact: Your credit report is really your credit history. It's great that you've made those payments, but this information will stay on your report for seven years. However, lenders do weigh more recent activity more than older payment history.

Myth: My divorce decree will take precedence over a credit obligation.

Fact: Credit obligations outweigh a divorce decree. You will still be held responsible for those payments if you incurred the debt jointly.

Myth: Lenders will only consider my credit score when deciding whether or not to loan me money.

Fact: They will also consider your salary, your employment history, and the amounts of other debt that you have. However, credit scores do play a large part in the decision. One exception to this is obtaining a mortgage. The closer the credit score to 800, the better the odds of getting a loan only on your credit score.

Myth: My credit score will improve if I close out all my old cards that I don't really use any more.

Fact: Closing an account sometimes may have an adverse effect on a credit score. Credit scoring looks at the total availability of credit you have at your disposal and how much you have spent against it. If your credit available on all cards adds up to $50,000, for example, and you have only spent $5,000 of that, it looks great on your credit report. On the other hand, if you have closed all of the credit cards exclusive of one, and the limit on that card is $7,500, that same $5,000 worth of debt would decrease your credit score because you would have exceeded more than thirty-five percent of the credit available to you.

Myth: I know poor credit will affect me financially, but it won't be an issue in any other part of my life.

Fact: These days, about seventy percent of employers are checking credit reports before making offers to hire, since they have found that people with money problems are more likely to call in sick, have problems at home, or steal.

Myth: If I get in over my head with credit, I can always file for bankruptcy protection.

Fact: The bankruptcy laws are getting tougher, and it is likely that eventually, you will have to pay back much of the debt anyway. It is much better to negotiate with your creditors to arrange a long-term payment plan. Bankruptcy stays on your credit report for ten years!

Myth: It is okay to go over your credit limit if the store accepts it. This must mean that the credit card company authorized the purchase.

Fact: Never go over your credit card limit. First, you will be hit with a late fee of $25 or more. Second, the credit card company will raise your interest rate sky high. Third, you could lose as much as eighty points off your credit score.

Myth: I should just avoid using credit cards all together.

Fact: Creditors hold it against you if you have no credit history almost as much as if you have a poor history. You need to have at least one card that you make purchases with each month, and then pay the balance off each month. If you are an uncontrolled spender, ask for a very low credit limit and keep a notebook to record all that you are spending each month.

Myth: My credit is so bad now, it will be destroyed forever.

Fact: If you start paying your bills on time and controlling your spending today, you will be well on your way to repairing your credit history. Scoring systems look much more closely at your recent activity than at the distant past, and your credit history only shows the past seven years, and bankruptcy for ten years.

The subject of the next chapter is the FICO Score, the score that most lenders use in determining your credit worthiness. In this chapter, I will analyze this credit scoring system and give instruction on how to get your credit report for review.

CHAPTER 2

Your FICO Score:
The Key to the Credit Chest

You can close the windows and darken your room,
and you can open the windows and let light in.
It is a matter of choice. Your mind is your room.
Do you darken it or do you fill it with light?

—Remez Sasson

If you're going to win at the credit game and build wealth, you will have to play by the lenders' rules. However, this does not mean you can't use the system to your advantage. Let's take a look at the main method everyone employs to evaluate your ability to pay back the money you want to borrow.

A Fair Isaac and Company (FICO) credit score with report is used by most banks, credit card companies, landlords, insurance companies, and even employers. This credit scoring system was named after two men—engineer Bill Fair and mathematician Earl Isaac—who pioneered the formula to predict who would be at risk for nonpayment. The report shows in vivid detail your bill-paying history and all your current debts. Most of the time, lenders will ask for your permission to pull your credit report, but not always.

Everyone is assigned a number known as the credit score, and the numbers range from 300 to 850. The higher the score, the better the chance you have to secure a loan. Not only will you be approved for credit if you keep your score high (above 700), but you will also receive the lowest possible interest rates. If your credit score is low due to paying bills late or having too much outstanding debt, you get the double whammy of being denied credit or paying outrageous interest rates, which get you further into debt. We will be going into great detail on how to improve your score in Chapter Five.

Whatever your credit score is, be assured that it is not the only thing lenders consider when making a decision on a loan request. They will also consider your current salary, whether you own your home, how long you've lived there, the amount of equity in your home, etc. However, your credit score is a major factor.

There is a positive side to lenders relying on the FICO report score in making a credit decision. First of all, it eliminates a lot of discrimination that used to go on in the not-so-distant past. Women were frequently turned down for credit unless their husbands cosigned the loans; many minorities were outright rejected based on the color of their skin; and students were not even considered. Today, you can apply for a loan from your PC or telephone, and within seconds, the lender can look up your credit score and make an instant decision. Of course, sometimes, this process is a little too easy!

The other benefit of the universal reliance on credit scoring by lenders is that your older credit transactions do not count as much as your current ones. If you had a poor payment history several years past, it will not stay with you forever. Credit agencies only report activity for the past six years, bankruptcies for 10 years, and unpaid tax liens for fifteen years.

The very first step toward getting out of debt, cleaning up your credit history, and investing in your future is to request a copy of the credit report that everyone else is looking at. It will be a bit of a challenge to fix any errors—and you can't erase your entire past but you will be laying a great foundation for moving forward.

How Credit Is Monitored

Every time you use a credit card or take out a mortgage or any other type of loan, this information is automatically reported to the three major credit scoring corporations: Equifax, Experian, and Trans-Union. In addition, every time you pay a bill, whether it is on time or not, that data is reported. It is interesting to note, however, that some types of payments are not reported to the credit scoring companies, including:

Medical bills
Utility bills
Legal bills
Personal loans from friends and family
Rent

You will want to keep this in mind when deciding which bills to pay first if you are in a credit crunch. Methods for debt reduction are presented in Chapter Seven.

The Big Three

Here is the contact information for the "big three" credit reporting agencies. Believe it or not, the information on your reports might be slightly different on each one. This is due to the different ways the credit scoring companies collect and report their information and that is why it is a good idea to obtain copies of your report from all three agencies every year. Most lenders will use the middle score when evaluating a credit application.

Equifax
P.O. Box 740241
Atlanta, GA 30374
800-685-1111
http://www.equifax.com

Experian (formerly TRW)
P.O. Box 2106
Allen, TX 75013-2106
888-397-3742
http://www.experian.com

TransUnion Corporation
P.O. Box 403
Springfield, PA 19064-0403
800-888-4213
http://www.transunion.com

How to Get a Copy

You will need to get a little "anal" about receiving and monitoring your credit report on a regular basis. By law you are able to receive a free copy of your report from each of the big three reporting agencies every year. So, here's how to monitor your report every four months without spending any money.

In month one, order a report from Equifax, either by calling, writing, or making an online request. Four months later, order one from Experian, and four months after that, get one from TransUnion. This way you will be able to see that corrections have been made, that requested accounts have been closed, and that there is no identity theft going on. Though using this method will get you a free report quarterly, there is a risk. The risk is that the credit reporting agencies don't always report the same information about you in their file. When you pull one report independent of the other two, you will run the risk of missing information that is only reported by one of the other agencies.

If you are denied credit, a new job, or an insurance policy based on information obtained from your credit report, you have the right to request a free copy of your report within sixty days. In addition, if you are on public assistance, or are unemployed and plan to look for a job in the next sixty days, you can get a free copy.

So, don't delay. It's time to face the music and take that first big step toward improving your credit history by getting a copy of your credit report. Next, you need to understand all the information you are faced with on the report. To assist you with understanding and reading a credit report, a copy of a TransUnion's TrueCredit report can be found on my website, www.theroadtocreditrepair.com.

How to Read Your Credit Report

A credit report has four main sections:

Section A: Identifying Information
This section includes your name, address, Social Security number, telephone number, date of birth, and current

and previous employers. This information is not used in calculating your score, but rather as a means to identify you. You will make life easier for yourself if you always use the same complete, legal name in all your business and employment transactions.

Section B: Public Record and Collection Items

A potential lender wants to know if there are any legal judgments against you. Information gathered from state and county records will include any court-ordered payments, divorce settlements, bankruptcies, foreclosures, lawsuits, wage attachments, liens, and other judgments. In addition, this section will report any overdue payments from collection agencies.

Section C: Credit Payment History

This section will report your payment history—both positive and negative—on your car loans, credit cards, mortgage, and any personal loans from financial institutions. If the numbers don't match the current status of your accounts, that's because the information on a credit report can be as much as three months behind. Each listing will also include the date you opened the account, the credit limit or loan amount, and the "current" balance.

Section D: Inquiries

Potential lenders also want to know how many other companies have requested your credit report. Their thinking is, if a lot of other companies are looking at your report, perhaps you are requesting too much credit and will get into too much debt. The report will include inquiries for the past two years.

Your FICO Score

Once my credit scores hit rock bottom, it wasn't until I monitored my credit report on a regular basis, fixed mistakes, worked with my creditors, and paid off my debts that I was able to improve my score.

The credit score is calculated using various types of information gathered from your report, which is then compared to hundreds of thousands of other reports, to predict who will be at risk for non-payment. As I mentioned previously, in order to obtain credit, you must first have used credit. Your report must show at least one loan or credit card account that has been opened for six months or more. There should also be some activity on that account during the past six months. So even if you put money in the bank, take out a loan, and pay it back from that account, this will satisfy the requirements for a credit history.

There are five main categories of information that FICO scores cover and each category is given a different weight or level of importance.

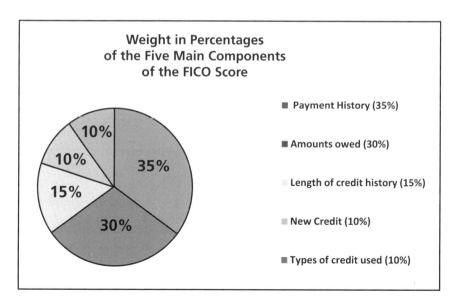

Here are some details about each.

Payment History (thirty-five percent of your credit score) One of the most important factors in calculating your credit score is whether or not you pay your bills on time. If you have been unable to pay bills in the past, a lender will be genuinely concerned that you will not be able to pay them in the future. However, your score does take into consideration how late your payments were. Obviously it is far worse to pay a bill ninety days late than thirty days. Also, a thirty-day late payment made recently will hurt you more than a ninety-day late payment four years ago. The following chart depicts how the FICO scoring model weighs payment history. As can be seen from the chart, the older the debt, the less impact it has on the credit score. This is one of the reasons why it is important to keep recent credit history current. Always rank debt prior to paying it off so that the impact on the credit score is minimized.

LENGTH OF CREDIT	IMPACT ON CREDIT SCORE
Most recent 12 months	40%
Prior 12 to 24 months	30%
Prior 24 to 36 months	20%
Prior 36 to 48 months	10%
Older than 4 years	0%

The good news is that if you pay your accounts on time, this will increase your score. A further note: a one-hundred-percent perfect payment record does not automatically give you a perfect credit score—as we will see.

Amounts Owed (thirty percent of your credit score)
If you owe a lot of money to many different creditors, this will affect your credit score no matter how much income you have. Lenders fear that you will be overextended and that if there is some kind of financial emergency, such as a job loss, you will be unable to pay all your bills. If you are in this situation, one way to improve your score is to use no more than thirty-five percent of the available credit on each account. In other words, if you have a Visa card with a $5,000 credit limit, don't spend more than $1,750 of that. If you need a $5,000 credit limit, you are better off taking out an additional card and keeping that limit under thirty-five percent of its limit as well.

Length of Credit History (fifteen percent of your credit score) The longer your (good) credit history, the better, but people who have short credit histories can get good scores if everything else in the report is positive. Lenders also want to see some activity on at least one of your accounts every six months.

New Credit (ten percent of your credit score) You do not want to open several new credit accounts within a short period of time, especially if you do not have a long credit history. Your credit score will reflect how many inquiries have been made about your credit report, but the system does allow for multiple inquiries for one new account. For example, if you are shopping for a loan on a new car or a potential mortgage, numerous inquiries will be made for your credit report before you can be quoted a rate.

You will not be penalized if multiple inquiries show up on your report if it is within a short period of time.

Types of Credit in Use (ten percent of your credit score) This category looks at the mix of credit cards, car loans, personal loans, retail accounts, and mortgage loans that you have, as well as your total number of accounts. You do not have to have one of each type, but it is a good idea not to over extend yourself by having too many credit accounts.

VantageScore

In a surprise move, the three major credit bureaus got together and announced in March 2006 a new scoring system they designed to rival the hold the FICO system has on the market. They claim it is more consistent than the FICO system and that it will help more people qualify for credit. Others claim that the big three are only pushing VantageScore because they are tired of paying a fee to FICO every time they issue a credit report.

While FICO scores range from 300 to 850, VantageScore ranges from 501 to 990. They provide letter grades which I liken to those we received in elementary school:

> 901–990: A credit
> 801-900: B credit
> 701-800: C credit
> 601-700: D credit
> 501–600: E credit

Studies comparing the FICO system and VantageScore have found the same percentages of people in their highest three tiers.

While there are more tiers in the middle of the FICO system, about the same percentage of people fall into the lowest levels in both systems. However, there is some evidence that borrowers who have fairly decent scores in FICO would have lower scores in VantageScore.

At this time, it is questionable that very many banks and other financial institutions will adopt the VantageScore system in the near future. They have invested millions in setting up the FICO scoring system and would have to start all over to convert to something new. However, the basic guidelines of keeping your score high remain about the same for both systems: paying your bills on time, reducing your debt, and not closing old accounts.

Fixing Mistakes

Experts estimate that anywhere from twenty-five to forty percent of credit reports contain errors. Don't let yours be one of them! Mistakes could range from having the wrong name or an incorrect Social Security number to showing activity on a credit card you never use, or worse, massive theft from someone stealing your identity. Or there could be some important information missing such as the fact that you paid off a tax lien.

This is why it is crucial to obtain a copy of your report on a regular basis and schedule time each week to work on correcting errors until your credit score improves. In Chapter Five we will discuss exactly how to handle each type of negative information or mistake and how to improve your credit score step by step.

CHAPTER 3

Getting Credit
for the First Time

*Beginning on the right road is not nearly as important
as finishing the journey, and finishing it successfully.
Visualize your goals clearly, add desire and faith,
and you will surely achieve them.*

—REMEZ SASSON

It used to be that if you did not have credit established, it was difficult to have banks and department stores grant you credit if you were inexperienced paying back money borrowed on credit. It was like applying for a job, and being turned down because you were inexperienced—even though you knew you could do it.

There was, however, one department store in town that would give a credit card to someone without a credit history. All you had to do was send in a copy of your degree, proving that you had completed college and credit was granted. With the demonstrated responsibility of using that card wisely, you had an opportunity to get other cards.

Today we are bombarded with credit card offers all the time. It is far too easy now to get a credit card. It seems as though credit card companies are hoping that you will get in over your head and run up all kinds of debt. Meanwhile, we hear the advice of so-called experts, who tell us to live on cash, never use credit, and only take out a loan for a mortgage. It takes a while to make it to this level. Even if you were there, your credit score would not grow because you would not have the essentials reported in your credit profile, which the models need to generate a good score.

Case in point: My aunt, who lived in southern Louisiana, needed to get a home-improvement loan for some major repairs at her home. She owned her home and bought everything with cash. The department store credit card in her name had a zero balance and had been in this state for many years. Had it not been for the housing department in the city underwriting the loan, she never would have been approved. It is imperative to keep a balance of good credit reporting in your credit profile. My friend hit the nail on the head when she joked that managing your credit score is like having a full-time job.

Every day people are rejected for loans because they don't owe a dime to anyone and have never missed paying a utility bill on time. The truth of the matter is, you need to prove to the FICO scoring system that you can manage and use revolving loans maturely and that you can pay your installment loans as agreed. The system is designed to dissect credit transactions to determine if you are paying your bills on time monthly. If there is nothing to analyze, your credit score will be negatively affected because you don't have a credit history that conforms to the model that the FICO scoring system is designed to interpret.

So if you are one of those who never receives credit offers, how do you establish credit for the first time? Read on!

Ways to Establish First-time Credit

Send in a copy of your college degree with an application. Often, you can get a credit card based on your earning of a college degree.

If you have a college student loan you are way ahead of graduates who don't, as far as getting credit. These loans are reported to the credit bureau. A student loan can be a great advantage, if you keep it current. Be sure to avoid a default.

Apply for an unsecured credit card. Department store and gas company cards are usually the easiest to get. Use the cards for three months and make payments on time. Then apply for Visa, MasterCard, etc., which will increase your credit potential.

Apply for a secured credit card. In essence, with these, you deposit the money into an account, make your expenditures, and then pay yourself back. It's credit with training wheels, but it does prove that you can make responsible credit purchases and make payments on time.

Try for a small loan via your local credit union. The interest rates might be higher since you are applying for the first time, but the plan right now is to get credit and begin establishing a history.

Open a bank account, if you don't have one. Credit applications ask if you have an account. Have the bank issue you a Visa- or MasterCard-type debit card. You can use the debit card when applying for instant credit in a department store that offers instant credit with proof of a major credit card.

If you don't think you would qualify for credit in your own name, start by asking a friend or family member to cosign the loan. Both of you will then be responsible for paying back the loan. The benefit to you is that you will have started a credit history. Be sure to pay according to the terms of the loan because when someone cosigns for you, they are guaranteeing that you will responsibly pay back the loan. To do this, they put their creditworthiness on the line. Always be cognizant that if you are irresponsible in repaying the loan, and they don't have the ability to make the payments, their credit score will suffer. As soon as you can, try to get credit in your name only.

A special note to women: It used to be that if you were married, credit was issued partially to the husband, especially if the wife was a stay-at-home mom. If you are in this situation, get at least one credit card in your name only! If, God forbid, you are ever widowed or divorced, you will want to have a credit history in your own name. Single women and career women normally do not have problems obtaining credit as long as their ability to repay has been demonstrated.

Congratulations! You are now on the road toward establishing a healthy credit score. In later chapters, we will talk about what to do when you get in over your head and get involved in the bad side of credit. As you move forward, remember these words of William E. Henley: "I am the master of my fate; I am the captain of my soul." Now that you are establishing credit, just remember how easy it is to become entrapped.

In the next chapter, we will discuss how to protect your credit from identity theft.

CHAPTER 4

Prepare to Fight Identity Theft

Honesty pays,
but it doesn't seem to pay enough
to suit some people.

—KIN HUBBARD

Can you imagine what it would be like to have always paid your bills on time, never to have taken out more credit than you could afford, and to have paid your taxes your entire adult life, only to apply for a loan and be rejected? Can you imagine this happening to you after you've taken the time to repair your credit? Think how you would feel if you found out that someone has stolen your identity and has gone on quite a spending spree with your credit. In one fell swoop, your sterling reputation could be ruined; your hard work set back.

Recently, a man in Winchester, Virginia was surprised to receive a $2,800 check from his bank for overpayment on his second mortgage. Even more baffling was that he didn't have a second mortgage!

It turned out that just from having his wallet stolen, someone was able to buy a $419,000 townhouse with no money down in his name!

This has been happening more and more lately as thieves as well as hackers get more sophisticated. To add insult to injury, some family members cannot even be trusted around your Social Security number.

This subject reminds me of how I became a victim of identity theft. One summer, I opened my home to my cousin and his wife—rolled out the red carpet, even. We had a wonderful time reminiscing about our childhood years. It felt good to have had them for the weekend.

However, the feeling was short-lived when an unauthorized credit card charge from a jewelry store appeared on my bill and then, out of the blue, I received a credit card from a department store without my making an application for it. As if this were not enough, another of my creditors wrote to inform me that my request to have my credit limit increased was approved. This happened during the early '80s when computers weren't as sophisticated as they are now. It took several days for the instant credit to appear. Almost a month went by before I was even notified of the disaster.

I was not as savvy then as I am now with credit repair, but I knew enough to surmise that a credit card company would not just arbitrarily send out credit cards and raise limits without someone asking. So I called them up and I found out, through a name used as a reference on the application, that my cousin's wife had stolen my identity and lived it up in a border town in South Texas for a weekend—to the tune of over $3,000.

Quickly, I got to work repairing the damage! I did not hesitate to call the police and file a report. I am happy to report that because I acted quickly and precisely, the damage did not set me back more than a few days. The moral of the story is this: If credit is granted to you and you did not ask for it, then something is up. Pay attention to the signs and investigate. It may stop severe damage to your credit reputation.

With identity theft we risk losing out on job opportunities, great insurance rates, great interest rates, government security clearances, or any type of loan because of fraudulent information that lands on our credit reports. In extreme cases, we could even be charged with crimes. However, the good news is that our banks and credit card companies are just as anxious to stop and prevent identity theft as we are. If you can prove identity theft, you will not be held liable for payments on items purchased by someone who stole your credit information. Unfortunately, it sure is a pain to clean up the mess and this is an understatement.

We need to stay on our toes every day, doing our part to prevent identity theft. This chapter will describe in detail what to do if you are a victim, and how to prevent it from happening in the first place.

How Thieves Steal Our Identities

Burglaries, robberies, and pick-pocketing lead to most identity theft cases and sixty percent of them are committed by friends or relatives, according to Professor William Kresse, who has studied identity fraud. In addition to good, old-fashioned theft of mail and wallets, here are other ways thieves try to obtain your personal financial information:

> **Diving into dumpsters and trash cans.** Believe it or not, people do this and find valuable information on your old bills and bank statements.

> **Sending change of address forms to your creditors so your billing statements go to them.** From there, they have all of your account information and it will take a while for you to notice.

Using a special storage device when processing your credit card purchases is called "skimming." This device is used by thieves to copy all of your credit card information.

"Phishing." This occurs when thieves send you emails that look like they are from either your bank or credit card company to get you to reveal your personal financial information. I received one from PayPal not too long ago telling me that I had to update my password on a particular Website. The email looked just like it came from the real company.

"Pretexting." Thieves use the pretext of being an official from a company that requires information from your bank, a telephone company, or a retail store. For example, someone pretends they are calling your bank from the local telephone company saying they have a refund to send you but don't have your current address. They might add that you authorized a direct deposit but gave them an incorrect account number and then ask the bank to clarify the correct one.

Asking to use your cell phone and using it to call a number that has caller ID. This technology is good in some cases and bad in others. When they get to the phone that they dialed from your number, they simply use the Internet to perform a reverse lookup and they have your address. This leads to more channels where they can acquire even more information about you.

Think it can't happen to you? Think again. Fortunately there are easy steps we can all take in our daily lives to help prevent identity theft.

Ten Things You Should Never Do

Leave bills you are paying in your mailbox for the mail carrier to pick up. It's very easy for someone to drive by, notice the red flag, and steal your payment, along with your credit card number or other identifying information. Go the extra distance and put all mail in an official mailbox or stop in at the post office. Be sure to have your mail held at the post office whenever you will be out of town. Likewise, don't write your account number on the outsides of envelopes.

Sell or dispose of a computer without totally erasing the hard drive. Anyone with any knowledge of computer hardware can easily get information right off there.

Carry credit cards you rarely use, your Social Security card, your birth certificate, your green card or your passport—unless it's absolutely necessary. It is too easy to have them lost or stolen.

Let anyone write your home phone number on a check. And certainly don't have it preprinted. Did you know that with Google, you can type in a phone number and get the person's name and address? You're better off using a debit card rather than checks. However, if that doesn't work for you, give out a work phone number or your spouse's if one is needed on the check.

Say your credit card number out loud on the phone if you are in a public place. Thieves have very good hearing. Also, be cautious when punching in a phone card number on a pay phone or entering your PIN number at an ATM. "Shoulder surfers" are out there watching.

Allow your name to be part of a list to receive pre-approved offers. It is very easy for a thief to steal the envelope, sign you up for the card, and give a new address. To prevent this from happening to you, simply call 1-888-5OPTOUT (888-567-8688) or go to OptOutPrescreen.com to have your name removed from credit bureau marketing lists.

Type in your credit card or Social Security number on the Internet, unless it is on an encrypted site. The Internet address bar will show "https," and a padlock symbol will appear at the bottom of the browser window. This applies to mentioning a credit card number in an e-mail as well.

Give out personal or credit card information over the phone unless you know exactly to whom you are talking, such as an airline or catalogue company that you called. This applies to charities as well. Send them a check after you have examined their literature and then you will have a good record when it comes time to do your taxes. Criminals also "phish" for victims by calling or e-mailing to "verify" account numbers or passwords. Official businesses do not obtain information this way.

Open any attachments on e-mails from unfamiliar people. Once hackers have access to your system they can do all sorts of damage.

Use a debit card when making purchases on the Internet or over the phone. I know someone whose checking account was wiped out after she used her debit card instead of a credit card.

How to Prevent Identity Theft—
Ten Things You Should (Or Must) Do

Invest in a shredder. To avoid any chance of someone raiding your garbage cans to look for identifying information about you (again, there are people out there who do this for a living), get in the habit of shredding all of your mail and any other documents that bear your name, address, etc. I have two shredders in my home: one in my office and one where I open the mail. I scrutinize trash to ensure no one in my household can be identified before I discard it. If it has any identifying information on it, I shred it. You can tear up everything before you toss it into the trash; however, you can't do it as well as a shredder.

Protect your Social Security number like it's gold. With this number a thief can get just about anything in your name—passport, driver's license, apartment, credit cards, etc. Never put it on your driver's license or health plan card. When you write a check or purchase alcohol everyone wants to see your license.

Check your bills and bank statements as soon as they arrive. The earlier you can detect an error or theft, the quicker you can repair the damage. Call the lender if bills do not arrive on time.

Memorize your Social Security card and passwords. More on password selection later.

Ask questions. Some stores request your telephone number just for their "mailing lists," while others want your driver's license number for no apparent reason. If a request for personal information seems inappropriate for the type of transaction you are making, ask why they need the information and how it will be used and protected. If all else fails, make up a number or shop elsewhere! Or do like I do and just say, "No." It is not their business and if it is used as a record key for their mailing list you don't need the extra mail and enticement to spend money anyway.

Install firewall, virus, and spyware software on your home computer. Only download free software from sources you know and trust. If you use Internet Explorer, set the browser security to at least "medium."

Secure your personal financial information in your home. Don't leave it lying around for roommates, your children's friends, housekeepers or repair people to see.

When you sign up for a new credit card, keep an eye on the calendar to make sure you receive it within an appropriate period of time. If you don't, call the company and ask if the card was sent, or if anyone has filed a change of address notice. Better yet, if you can afford it, purchase a postal box to receive all of your mail.

When you order new checks, ask if you can pick them up at your bank rather than have them delivered to your home address. Living in a rural area and traveling a lot, this is one of the things that I swear by. My checks are safer with my banker than they are in my mailbox.

By now, it should go without saying: **Send for your credit report at least twice a year and correct any errors immediately!**

What to Do If Identity Theft Happens to You

Okay. Someone stole your identity just as someone did mine. You found out because you finally got around to requesting a copy of your credit report, or perhaps because you were rejected for a loan, or received some unauthorized credit cards. You began to see all kinds of expenditures you never made, or maybe there were only one or two big ones. Worse yet, bill collectors started to call.

It's time to take immediate action. Here is a checklist of what you can do in order to start cleaning up the mess and restoring your good credit reputation.

Call the police and file a report stating that you have been the victim of identity theft. This is first and foremost because identity theft is a crime. Report your identity theft to the local police. Give them as many details as possible about what happened. They will take the report and provide you with a report number. In addition, the officer may give you forms to use in order to request account information from the creditors. Filing a police report legitimizes your claim. Besides, the credit agencies will ask if you filed a police report.

Notify the three major credit bureaus. First, give the three credit bureaus a call to let them know that you believe you are a victim of identity theft and ask them to put a fraud alert on your file. Give them the police report number. You will only be able to reach an automated telephone system and will have to enter your Social Security number and other identifying information. The fraud alert will prevent anyone from opening a new credit account in your name and the alert will stay on for ninety days. This alert can be extended for up to seven years once all the forms have been filed. The credit bureaus will then send you a letter confirming the fraud alert and what your next steps should be. There is no charge to obtain additional copies of your credit report when you are a victim of identity theft. In the letter from each credit bureau will be a telephone number of the person to contact at the bureau who is in charge of fraud. Here are the numbers to call—and remember, you need to notify all of them:

Experian 1-888-397-3742

Equifax 1-800-525-6285

TransUnion 1-800-680-7289

Call the detective assigned to your case. Once you have received the forms and a copy of your credit report, contact the detective assigned to your case and describe all fraudulent information listed on your credit report. Provide a copy of your credit report from all three agencies. Black out any information such as other credit card numbers first. (You don't need to risk additional identity theft.) Chances are the detective probably will not be able to do anything unless you actually know who committed the crime. If a family member committed the crime, statistics show that the victim rarely reports the relative's name. Thus, in most cases, the crime goes unpunished.

Fill out the forms. Be sure to fill out and send the forms given to you by the police officer to the creditors affected by the identity theft along with the police report. If you receive any information back from the creditors, be sure and share it with the local police officer in charge of your case.

Notify your creditors. Your next step is to notify the creditors where the thief opened or used your accounts. Ask for the security or fraud department and tell them you are a victim of identity theft. Ask them to close any affected accounts and to report them to the credit bureaus as "closed at the consumer's request." It may not hurt to even have them add the word "FRAUD." Also, request that you not be held responsible for any new accounts that have been opened by the thief. If you need to reopen an account, have it set up to require a PIN number or password every time it is used. This is a huge inconvenience; however, it is absolutely necessary. The light at the end of the tunnel is that, in time, everything will go back to normal and all of the protective controls can be dropped. If unauthorized charges were made to an open account, have your creditor close the account and transfer all authorized charges to a new account.

Complete a theft affidavit. It is imperative that you fill out a form called the "Federal Trade Commission's ID Theft Affidavit." This form is available from my website: http:// www.theroadtocreditrepair.com. However, not all companies accept this affidavit. They may use an in-house version. If they don't send you one, contact each company to find out if they accept the FTC's affidavit. Send copies of the completed form to all your creditors where the thief opened accounts in your name, to the credit bureaus, and to the police. You may be wondering why it is that after all you have been through that you have to do this. Completing the affidavit will make certain that you do not become responsible for any debts incurred by an identity thief. To protect yourself you must prove to each of the companies where accounts were opened or used in your name that you didn't create the debt. It's a pain, but trust me, it works.

Put it in writing. Next, write a letter to all three credit bureaus, repeating what you reported in your phone call. (For a sample of a letter reporting identity theft to the credit bureaus, refer to my website, www.theroadtocreditrepair.com.)   Include copies of the police report and the completed ID Theft Affidavit. Remind the bureaus that they must remove any negative information that you claim is a result of identity theft. Send all information by certified mail with return receipt requested. Keep copies of everything. According to the FCRA, they have thirty days to verify your claim or to remove all disputed information. If you follow this procedure, your nightmare could be over in less than sixty days. You can also dispute fraudulent charges online with the credit bureaus at their websites, under "dispute":

> http://www.experian.com
> http://www.equifax.com
> http://www.transunion.com

Write to your creditors. You will also need to write to your creditors where accounts were opened or used fraudulently. (For a sample letter, refer to my website, www.theroadtocreditrepair.com.) Include a copy of the police report and the ID Theft Affidavit and black out any other credit card numbers.

Notify your banks. If you know your ATM card, checks, or other bank account information has been stolen, call the bank immediately and close your account. You will then have to open a new account with new passwords. Request that the bank notify its check-verification company; you should also notify the major ones that retail stores use. Tell them not to accept checks from your old account. The major companies include:

Chexsystems—800-428-9623
CrossCheck—800-843-0760
Equifax—800-437-5120
International Check Services—800-631-9656
TeleCheck—800-710-9898
Certegy—800-437-5120

You can also find out if bad checks have been written in your name by calling SCAN at 800-262-7771.

Notify the Department of Motor Vehicles. If your driver's license has been stolen, you should contact your local DMV office to report the theft and to put a fraud alert on your license. You should also arrange to change your license number when you apply for a new one.

Notify Social Security. If you believe your Social Security number has been stolen, call the Social Security Fraud Hotline at 800-269-0271. It is usually not a good idea to get a new Social Security number. First, the Social Security Administration rarely allows this, and second, you risk losing your credit history as well as your academic and military records.

Security Freezes

The latest method people are using to prevent or recover from identity theft is to put an official credit freeze on their credit reports. This means that potential creditors cannot get a copy of your report unless you temporarily lift the freeze. Some states now allow anyone to do this while others restrict it to those who are victims of identity theft.

Placing a credit freeze will not affect your credit score or your ability to obtain a copy of your own credit report. The cost is about $10 per credit freeze unless you are an identity theft victim, but you will need to pay the $10 to all three credit reporting agencies. Also, you will need to put a freeze on both your name and your spouse's, if you both have a credit history.

Under a credit freeze, several types of companies still have access to your credit report. These include creditors you are already doing business with, such as your mortgage company or credit card companies. Also, collection companies that do business with your current creditors will have access to your reports, as well as those who send out pre-screened credit card offers.

In some states, potential employers, insurance companies, landlords and other organizations not considered creditors can also access your reports while your credit freeze is on. Government agencies investigating child support payments, taxes, or medical fraud would also have access.

So who does that leave out under a credit freeze? In most cases when a freeze is in place, the creditor will contact you and verify your identity before issuing credit in your name.

The best use of a credit freeze is to prevent a thief from opening new accounts in your name. However, the thief would still be able to use your existing credit accounts and could open accounts such as telephone or bank accounts which do not usually request credit reports first.

You can lift the freeze at any time to allow a particular creditor to request your report or to specify a period of time when reports will be available. However, you will have to pay the credit bureaus each time you do this—usually around $10 or $12.

Unless you are an identity-theft victim, or fear you might become one if your wallet is stolen, it is probably not worth the time and expense to put a credit freeze on your reports. However, as identity theft becomes more prevalent, it is a decision we all may be facing in the near and distant future.

Creating Effective Passwords

Research has shown that the most profound way that unauthorized users get access to your computer, ATM, or other password-protected system is this—they guess your password. They either saw you type it in, found a piece of paper lying next to your computer, or used a very effective software program whose sole purpose is to guess passwords. Once they get in, they have access to your complete identity, including bank accounts, credit cards, and computer files.

When creating a new password, don't use words that can be easily figured out by another person. Rather, follow these guidelines and you will come up with some great ones:

Don't use personal information such as your birth date, your mother's maiden name, your middle name, your phone number, or your address. It's too easy for someone to figure these out.

Don't use any words that can be found in a dictionary. This includes places and famous people.

Make the password as long as possible. If there's room, use at least six letters and two numbers. Include a punctuation mark, as well as mixed uppercase and lowercase letters.

Don't use your account number for the password, and avoid characters that are easy to spot while being typed such as 12345. Furthermore, be conscious not to use all the same letters. Remember to combine numbers, special characters, and letters in a combination of upper and lower case. Passwords constructed of this mixture are generally considered strong.

Try using the first letter of each word in a phrase, such as, "I Will Always Love Texas" (IWALT). Other people have had success intentionally misspelling a word.

When creating a new password, make an effort to avoid names of family members, pets, associates and close friends. Also, never use a combination of words or characters that can be easily obtained, like your car tags, birthday, place of birth, street address, street name, and words that can be found in a dictionary.

How Often to Change a Password

Most experts recommend changing your password every thirty days. At most you should never wait longer than ninety days. Others say the more frequent, the better. In any case, don't reuse an old password and don't write it down anywhere that will be easy for someone else to find.

For some comprehensive information on identity theft, visit my website, www.theroadtocreditrepair.com, and click on Identiy Theft to download a brochure containing facts about identity theft.

Now that we have discussed how to prevent identity theft and what to do if it happens to you, let's move on to improving your credit score.

CHAPTER 5

Improve Your Credit Score— Start Today!

Though no one can go back and make a brand new start,
anyone can start from now and make a brand new ending.

— Carl Bard

When I worked as a software engineer, my credit scores were good. During that time money was not an issue. As a matter of fact, there was plenty and we used it like it was water running freely in a stream. We spent tons of money on hollow purchases—a term I affectionately use to refer to purchases that won't fertilize your money tree. Other than our house, we had no empowering assets. Empowering assets are those that will grow you a money tree.

Until I quit my job, things were going great. We had three things working: our house, good credit, and money. Aren't these the three things that you need to be happy in life? But after I quit my job everything changed. Money was not as plentiful and we were not prepared.

The nest egg we had established vanished because our spending patterns lacked discipline. Though our lifestyle changed, we did not change our spending habits to coincide with it, primarily because of the circle in which we traveled.

More and more, we needed to borrow money to do deals and pay bills. Money was going out faster than it was coming in. Our wonderful credit score was caught in a downward spiral as we put off Peter to pay Paul. Interest on money borrowed became our biggest debt. Borrowing money nontraditionally is an expensive endeavor.

When a project did not turn out successfully, we were in deep trouble. When that happened, we would just borrow more money to compensate for the losses. Our debt kept growing and growing. Our credit score was not only despicable, but embarrassing for two highly professional individuals.

However, the situation could have been rectified in a minute. How? Either of us could have gone back to work. The problem was that once we tasted the independence of being our own bosses, jobs were considered, but never seriously. Or we could have simply changed our spending habits, which is eventually what we did.

The road to debt recovery, inclusive of credit repair, is about changing the habits that caused the predicament you're in. It is also about recognizing your responsibility in creating that predicament.

Sometimes, hitting bottom is essential before we can see the way to fight back to the top. If nothing else, it is an eye-opener. Once our dream became more important to us than the hollow purchases we were throwing our money away on, we started to develop discipline in our spending habits. Once we were able to acknowledge the roles that we were playing in our debt troubles, we could see clearly how to begin the solution.

We set out to become creditworthy and we recognized that raising our credit scores and reducing our debt was the first step toward setting us free from the bondage of the hard-money lenders. With the appropriate strategy implemented over a ten-month period, our credit scores improved—my husband's from the low 500s to well over 700.

With my instruction and guidance, you too, will experience this success. Though it takes a lot of work and determination, the system has a lot going in your favor. Let's go step by step and see how you can improve your score starting today. The greatest action is to just get started. Let's get serious!

To finish the moment, to find the journey's end in
every step of the road…is wisdom.

RALPH WALDO EMERSON

Improving Your Credit Score and Turning Debt Into a Positive Net

The manner in which you turn debt into a positive net involves having the equity in your assets exceed the amount of debt that you owe. For example, if your total debt is $10,000, and you have assets with a value of $50,000, your net worth is $40,000. I only count assets that will appreciate in my net worth.

Because you are worth $40,000, at any time you can liquidate to pay off the $10,000 debt. If this occurs, your net worth will be a liquid $40,000. Are you getting the picture? The object is to have the total value of your appreciable assets exceed your debt. Remember, the debt will only be good debt—the kind that grows your money tree. With good debt, the asset has the potential to pay the note on the debt that you carry through a lease or rental agreement.

My husband and I built affordable housing below $165,000 during a time when money was free-flowing for affordable home purchases. A smart investor could take advantage of the "no money down" concept to purchase and warehouse real estate.

The real estate we purchased was acquired using OPM: other people's money. While this money was freely flowing, we took the opportunity to increase our net worth by purchasing real estate to hold and rent—to use as residual income—to make us money as we slept. How we did this will be touched on briefly in this book; however, it is the major subject of my sequel.

I can tell you this, however: If you want to make money while you sleep and have your assets appreciate simultaneously, real estate investing is the way to go. To be successful you will need good credit, money, and equity.

Until well into May of 2007, borrowers with credit scores as low as 500 were obtaining financing for mortgage loans, but only in the subprime markets. Obtaining a loan in the subprime market meant paying a much higher interest rate and extra points during closing. More often than not, to qualify, the borrower had to accept an ARM—an adjustable rate mortgage. These mortgages are not fixed. They will adjust when the introductory rate used to initiate the loan ends. At this time, the interest rate will either increase or decrease depending on the index used to establish the rate, and it will normally adjust every six months or annually depending on the index it uses to adjust.

I limit my discussion of ARMs because today, the housing market for these borrowers is not so great. In good faith, I prefer not to recommend a mortgage of this type. If you listen to the news, you know that one of the reasons why the market is in the shape it's in has to do with the ARMs that are adjusting homeowners right out of their homes. Most often when an ARM adjusts, the interest rate increases. This increase causes a house note to increase, and may jeopardize the ability to continue to afford the home.

Because of the high number of foreclosures, there is an abundance of real estate available for purchase, and at awesomely great prices.

Rule of thumb: When the housing market is bleak,
buy and hold until a better day.
Now is the time to increase your net worth by buying real estate.

This high rate of foreclosure creates a problem among the subprime lenders. The problem is, the subprime market has collapsed. Too much money is being lost. Thus, to buy real estate now, you have to demonstrate your creditworthiness. It is very difficult to qualify for a mortgage loan without any money down. If you are a first-time homebuyer, there are still a few programs out there with down-payment assistance. The best place to look for these is in the Housing Department in the city in which you live.

My goal in assisting you with credit repair is to get you to the stage where you can start building wealth through real estate. Together we're going to turn your debt into a positive net. The best way to do this is to *just get started!*

We will take an aggressive approach to raising your credit score. It will take a lot of your time, money, and discipline. If you are not a homeowner, you will be prepared to become one. If you are a homeowner, you will be in a position to become a multiple property owner. If you are already a multiple property owner—a real estate investor— then you have arrived. However, you still have a reason for reading this book. It could be that your credit score is ailing, or you are stuck in the grasp of a hard-money lender. Either way, you will need a decent credit score and some cash reserve to improve on the position that you hold at the moment.

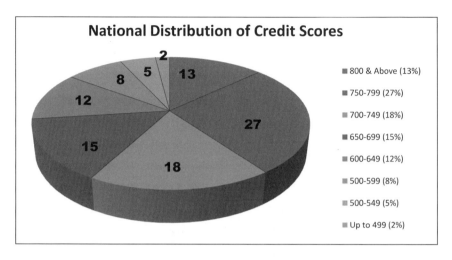

National Distribution of Credit Scores

- 800 & Above (13%)
- 750-799 (27%)
- 700-749 (18%)
- 650-699 (15%)
- 600-649 (12%)
- 500-599 (8%)
- 500-549 (5%)
- Up to 499 (2%)

What Credit Score Do You Want to Achieve?

There are two credit scoring systems that drive the industry today: the VantageScore system and the Fair Isaac Corporation's (FICO) score. You were given an overview of each in Chapter 2.

Since FICO is the most commonly used system in this country, we will limit our efforts to improving your FICO credit score.

The median FICO score in the U.S. falls right around 720. This is considered an excellent credit score. This means that most people in this country are creditworthy. ***Your goal is to get to the good or even the very good range—680 to 719. If, in the process, you top 720…congratulations!*** You will have arrived where most Americans are. With a score in this range, you should have no problem qualifying for a mortgage loan.

At 680, you will qualify for a decent mortgage loan, one that is considered "A" paper. You may be able to qualify for a one hundred percent loan to value (LTV), a ninety-five percent LTV, or a ninety percent LTV. This depends on how much equity is in the home and the standard for these loans set by the mortgage lender. When a lender grants a loan at ninety-five percent LTV, this means that five percent equity remains in the property. With a loan at ninety-percent LTV, ten percent equity remains in the property. Do you get the picture?

In addition, if you do not have a home, we will start you saving for a down payment on a mortgage loan by using the 10-20-70 plan. Yes, you will be saving while raising your credit score. I know this is going to take longer; however, it has to be. Just know that with patience and persistence, "you can do what you know needs to be done, as you have the power to do it"—these famous words, said by my uncle John, gave me the inspiration to persevere.

Saving money while you clean up your credit is an absolute necessity. With the 10-20-70 plan, you will be able to watch your nest egg grow. It may be slow and steady, but it will grow. Pretty soon, you will be able to fertilize your money tree.

There is a high price to pay if you are considered a poor credit risk. (We've beat this horse to death.) If you are approved for credit, that approval will have attached to it an outrageously high interest rate. You may think it is illegal to charge different people different rates, but based upon your credit history, lenders do have the right to charge a higher interest rate if they think you are a credit risk.

Legally, these interest rates can get excessively and abusively high. Because of this abuse, in 2006 the Department of Defense urged Congress to cap interest on loans marketed to the military at thirty-six percent. Thirty-six percent! Can you imagine that?

The reasoning of the lenders who assess such rates is this: It costs a lot of money to chase after someone for nonpayment. Their assumption is that the credit-scoring system that predicted your creditworthiness is one hundred percent accurate. It does not matter that some unusual circumstances, like losing a job or illness in the family, caused your credit problem. The algorithm that computes your credit score cannot think or feel. So, only the facts reported by your creditors are considered in the computation.

Thus to compensate for this risk, the repayment strategy is designed to keep you paying and repaying the money you borrowed over and over again. The system can almost be likened to indentured servitude: The high interest rates will enslave you for many, many years.

We are going to eliminate this debt. The goal is to have just three open lines of credit. However, as far as I am concerned, you can have more than three as long as all but two make money for you.

A word to the wise: If you want to have choices in your life, such as where and how you live, priority one is to take your current thinking patterns through a transformation that includes a desire to repair your credit history and improve your credit score. Next, you must start implementing changes in your lifestyle that will result in maintaining your improved credit score forever. The underlying formula for making this happen is debt reduction and decreased spending. What would also help is to pay the debt you do have on time and to work on a better balance within your debt-to-income ratio.

The Law and Your Rights

Before we get started on repairing the past, let's take a look at what the government has put in place in order to protect you as a consumer and to aid you in the reparation process.

The FICO credit scoring system used to be shrouded in mystery with borrowers having no idea what factors influenced their scores or what they could do if they were turned down for a loan. People were denied loans because of their race, religion, marital status, age—you name it.

Today that has all changed in YOUR favor. One of the most far-reaching laws that affected this is the Fair Credit Reporting Act (FCRA) of 1970 which has since been amended several times. The main goal of the law is to promote accuracy and to ensure that consumers have access to the same information about themselves that lenders, insurers, and employers can get from the credit bureaus. From my website, www.theroadtocreditrepair.com, you can download a copy of the FCRA. Print this document and study its contents.

The FCRA spells out how long negative information can be retained in your credit profile. It also requires the credit bureaus to investigate any information you believe is inaccurate and stipulates the timing the bureaus have to settle disputes. They affectionately refer to these disputes as "the reinvestigation process."

Section 611 of the FCRA, Procedure in Case of Disputed Accuracy outlines the procedure for verifying information in your credit file by the reporting agency. To facilitate the dispute of information that is reporting in your credit file, you can access my website, www.theroadtocreditrepair.com, to obtain sample letters that can be modified in your word processor to fit your situation, and then sent to the credit reporting agencies.

The bureaus have to resolve a dispute by the close of the thirtieth day from the date on which the dispute was received at the reporting agency. It is important to send all disputes to the reporting agency via certified mail. This is absolutely necessary! This proof will come in handy, especially if the file is not updated in the allotted time period. Certified mail or express mail can be tracked. Start tracking the letter the day after it is sent, taking care to record the name of the person that signed for the document. Once the document is received, the clock starts ticking.

On the thirtieth day, the reporting agency must have your file updated and the FCRA provides an additional five days for them to provide you with the results of the reinvestigation that you initiated. I know many individuals who have gotten lucky and had information removed from their credit files because the reporting agency was not in compliance with the FCRA. As a matter of fact, my husband was one of them.

Most companies use the Beacon score (Equifax credit) to determine creditworthiness. Equifax sent my husband's report to the wrong address after I sent them a certified letter updating the correct address in a dispute. This was a huge error and, likewise, a break for him. After the allotted time period expired, I pulled a copy of the report online, and noticed that the address was incorrect. As a matter of fact, it was not anywhere near our correct address.

The thought of the consequences of this error literally made me viscerally ill. I challenged them because there was no way my husband was going to receive his report per the auspices of the FCRA since it was mailed to the wrong address. As such, they were clearly in violation of Section 611(a)(6)—the section that dictates how the reporting agency reports to the consumer the results of the reinvestigation.

They did not want to adhere to the FCRA; however, after I threatened to sue because they had essentially exposed him to identity theft, they wiped all of the disputed debt from the report and, in an instant, his score jumped from 580 to 748. We now work like Trojans to keep it there. *Knowledge does have its privileges!*

Under the FCRA, you have the right to obtain a free copy of your report annually. This is important information because, often, individuals believe they have to pay the agencies to receive copies of the information reported in their credit files. Frequently, because they are charged, they never bother to pull copies of their reports and review the information contained in their files for accuracy. This is a bad habit that should be broken. At least once a year, you should be pulling a copy of your credit report from all of the major bureaus and scrutinizing what it contains. Immediately, you should issue a dispute to delete all erroneous information. I will show you how to do this later in this chapter under the section entitled: "Challenge Those Mistakes." However, first, let's look at disputing inquiries on your credit report.

The Truth about Inquiries

Sending a dispute to the credit bureaus to challenge an inquiry will not get you anywhere. You must dispute inquiries directly with the creditor who initiated the inquiry. Under the FCRA, the credit bureaus can only issue copies of your files when requested for what are called "permissible purposes." When an inquiry is made for your credit report, it is not the responsibility of the credit reporting agency to determine if the request is legitimate. As long as the creditors or people making the inquiry can demonstrate permissible purpose, they may have access to your information. Demonstrating permissible purpose is as simple as supplying an application with your identifying information. Nothing more!

Furthermore, the agency will only remove inquiries when instructed to do so by the originating creditor. Nevertheless, inquiries should be monitored, especially if a collection agency is contacting you for a debt that has exceeded the statute of limitation—the seven-year period that an agency can report a bad debt. Under these circumstances, the inquiry is not legitimate and should be challenged.

There are different types of inquiries. Some are considered "soft" because they don't affect your credit score such as an inquiry that is made to offer you a new credit card. Other inquiries will affect your score because you voluntarily agreed through a loan application to have the lender check your credit — such as when you initiate an application for a new car or a major credit card.

All inquiries remain on the credit report for twenty-four months. Remember inquiries associated with the hunt for a loan to purchase either a mortgage or a car loan will not alter your credit score.

Credit Denials and Your Rights

Another main focus of the law is protecting your rights after you are denied credit. First, if you are denied, the lender must provide you with the reason why within thirty days. The lenders can't say that they don't know why you were rejected because the credit bureau gives them up to four reasons as to why your score isn't higher. With that, at least, you will know the exact areas you need to work on in order to improve your credit score for the future.

Before attempting to raise your credit score, request your report to ensure you are working on the latest information in your file. Within sixty days of the denial, you have the right to request a free credit report from the three credit bureaus. You can try calling the bureaus and requesting the report over the phone. You only need to tell them that you were denied credit within the last sixty days. Give them the creditor that issued the denial, and they will forward your report. Obtaining a report under these circumstances is not the same as obtaining the free report that you are due annually. One does not have anything to do with the other. Any time you are denied credit, you have the right to a free credit report so that you can be aware of what information stopped you from receiving the credit.

Sometimes it is difficult to get through to a representative at the credit agency without a report number. If you do not have a current report number—one issued within the last ninety days—try using a number from a previous report. It will work as well; at least it does for me. Also, use the phone number that is listed on the report for contacting the agency. Otherwise you will either have to request the report in writing or request it from the website of the agency. In the latter case, you may or may not be able to obtain a free report. Remember, do not use this instance to obtain your annual free credit report. In case of a denial you have the right to receive a report regardless of any other received.

Now that you know what makes up your credit score, what your target score is, and your basic rights under the law, let's take a look at how we can increase that score.

Tips to Improve Your Credit Score— Today and Tomorrow

Whether you are experiencing a temporary financial crisis or you have an ongoing need to increase your credit score, this section is for you. I will give you specific steps to take to increase your score for both the short and long term.

Remember, if I can do it, you can too!
Just desire it and consistently work toward it.
Exhibit patience and perseverance, and it will happen!

Good Habits That Positively Influence Your Credit Score

The process of transforming your credit from bad to good is a tedious one. It will not happen overnight. Not only will it take time, but it will take money, too. Good habits should be adopted so that the transformation lasts over the long term.

Before you start the process, you should have an understanding of what factors—i.e., deadly sins—influence a reduction in your credit score. The do's and don'ts in the following list can start you on the road toward building a healthy credit history and a positive credit score.

1. Don't pay your bills late.

This is probably the number-one reason for getting a low FICO rating and, as we have seen, it represents thirty-five percent of your score. Lenders fear that if you did not pay someone else, there is an increased risk you will not pay them.

If you cannot make a payment on time, try to negotiate with the lender. If you come to an agreement, be sure to get it in writing and request that the late payment not be reported to the credit bureaus. Chances are the answer will be, "No!" However, it doesn't hurt to try.

Here's a tip to remember if you have no choice but to pay late: The credit bureaus do not record negative history unless the payment has exceeded more than thirty days from the due date. If the payment is due on the first, it will not be reported late as long as the payment is received before the first of the next month. So if you are sending more than one payment at a time, catching up a previous bill for whatever reason, and it is your fault, then you are late on your payment. This late payment, if reported, lowers your credit score. In addition, if any payment goes past the due date, you will be assessed a late charge.

Don't worry about the late charge if you have limited funds. If you do not pay it, it will be tacked onto the principal. Concentrate on making the payment. Just be sure that it reaches the lender before the due date of the next payment. A payment sent past the due date, but within the thirty-day period that it is due, will not bring down the credit score. The fact that the payment was not received in the thirty-day period has that honor.

Here's an example: Sarah has an auto loan with IOU Motors that is due on the first of each month. She is doing great until her son becomes sick which forces her to lose four days of work without pay. Her check is short and the due date for the car payment comes and goes. She does not have the money and she misses the payment on the date that it is due.

She manages to get in some overtime and receives some extra income on the twenty-seventh of the month. Now she has enough money to make the overdue payment as well as the next payment. Although she has missed the pay date, she can still save her credit score by sending the late payment before the due date of the next payment rolls around.

To accomplish this, she can overnight the payment via certified express mail to IOU Motors who should receive it by the twenty-eighth, or she can pay it online or over the phone. Generally, making a payment either online or on the phone will cause the payment to post immediately. However, these payments may incur additional charges.

Notice that I did not advise sending the payment via your bank's Bill Pay program. Though this is a convenient method to pay— one I use often—I would not trust the bank to send the payment such that it reaches the lender in time to prevent a 30 day late from posting to the credit bureaus. With something this important, you must handle it directly—without the middle man.

She can even call them to get instructions on a quick-collect payment through Western Union. The goal is to get the payment to the lender before the next payment comes due. If she can do this, her credit will not reflect a derogatory entry and the credit score will remain intact. She only has to pay the payment due, not the penalty for paying late. Though it is owed per the guidelines of the lender, it does not have to be collected, and it can wait until the final principal payment is made.

2. Don't charge more than thirty-five percent of your credit limit.

First and foremost, charge cards are a "no no"! They do nothing to fertilize the money tree, except when they are used to make business purchases that will make money for you. My advice: Cut them up while eliminating your debt. Cut them up but don't close the accounts. Not yet, anyway!

For all types of revolving credit cards, make every effort to keep the balance below thirty-five percent of the credit limit. Period. If you have a $1,000 limit on your Visa card, take care to ensure that the balance never exceeds $350. This is considered a low balance. You are better off having several cards with low balances rather than one that is very close to the credit limit.

3. Do use caution when combining your credit debt into one low-interest card.

A point to note: To acquire additional credit cards to play the "transfer the debt" game to a zero-percent interest card, you will have to create an inquiry on your credit which will drop your score a little. Moreover, you have to be careful that the transfer of the debt does not cause the debt to become unbalanced, which will also drop the credit score. Unless it is absolutely necessary, forget about creating more credit.

Perhaps you are playing the credit game of taking advantage of all the low or zero-percent interest credit card offers that come in the mail if you've any kind of decent credit history. You combine all the balances on your high-interest cards onto the new credit card, right up to the credit limit. Then when that card's rate goes back up after an initial period, you transfer the debt to another card, and the process begins again.

This method does have its advantages in that you will be paying down your debt faster, but only if you can totally eliminate the debt during the free interest rate period. If not, there are significant disadvantages that you need to know. While the zero-percent interest rate affords the opportunity for all payments to lower the principal balance, this method of debt reduction has a very negative effect on your credit score because the debt on the new card is at its maximum limit. As we have seen, FICO looks at how much you have spent compared to the credit limit on each card or loan. If you close an account once the funds are transferred, that lowers your amount of available credit when compared against the amount of debt you have.

Be careful to read the fine print on the terms and conditions for receiving the lower interest rate. A friend of mine transferred her debt to one card and then carelessly charged gas on the card because she was too lazy to search for her gas card. Unfortunately, she did this before reading the fine print. When the bill came, she noticed that the great interest rate she was given had increased. Why? One of the conditions to maintain the lower interest rate on the balance transfer was that there would be no charges on the card until the date of the lower interest rate period expired. Can you imagine that? Because of a $50 gas purchase, she lost a six-month, zero-percent interest rate on the debt she'd transferred.

Would you like to know what the new interest rate was? Well, it jumped to twenty-two percent. She called the company and talked until she was blue in the face, but to no avail. The rate on the penalty was higher than the eighteen-percent APR she had been paying before the transfer. To correct the problem, she paid the card company the amount of the balance transfer. The moral of the story is to remember to read the fine print on those too-good-to-be-true offers.

In some instances the balance transfer option may be extremely advantageous. If the goal is to increase the credit score by reducing the debt on the card to less than a third, transferring a portion of the debt may be advantageous if the deal on the interest rate is great. Believe it or not, it is better to have two cards below thirty-five percent of the credit limit than it is to have one card with no available credit left on it.

Though this may possibly work to improve your credit score, be sure you are disciplined enough not to dig a deeper hole. You could end up with two cards at the maximum limit. A much better and safer approach is to find a way to increase your income so you can pay off your debt for good. Later in this book, you will be given tips and strategies on how to reduce your debt using funds from extra income.

4. Don't put too much debt on retail credit cards.

For some reason, the credit scoring system rates third-party credit cards from department stores, furniture stores, electronics stores, etc., lower than the major credit cards such as Visa and MasterCard. You are better off closing these retail accounts and using your cards from the major credit card companies. Just remember to keep your balances around thirty-five percent of the credit limit for the card. Caution: Be sure not to cause a drop in your credit score because you closed those retail accounts. Remember, length of credit history has value as well, especially if the account has been in good standing for a number of years. Thus, if a credit history has not been established for the newly acquired major credit card, do not close those retail accounts if their credit history has been positive for more than 2 years. Pay them off; however, don't close them until you establish a good credit history for the major credit card.

5. Do monitor your credit report regularly.

Although the credit reporting agencies use computers to maintain data in your credit file, an individual has to enter the data. Because we are human, mistakes in data entry can occur. There can even be a coding error in the algorithm that processes the data entered.

The FCRA stipulates that all information reported in your credit file must be one-hundred-percent accurate. So make it a point to check your credit file and dispute all inaccuracies at least annually. There is no need for your credit health to suffer due to inaccurate information being reported.

Inaccurate information may be disputed directly with your creditor; however, the fastest and most assured way to have inaccuracies removed is to have the reporting agencies contact the creditor. Why? The reporting agency is bound by the FCRA. They will make every effort to comply within a thirty-day window; the negative information will be deleted if the verification is not completed within this timeframe. If, for instance, a creditor reports your credit limit at $0, and your balance is $1,000, your credit score will take a hit because of this mistake.

However, if you do not monitor your credit report, you will never know this until you apply for credit. An error like this may take up to fifty days to correct if disputed outside of the credit bureau. In the interim, you may not be granted the credit that you seek. Just remember to dispute errors with each national reporting agency simultaneously.

Erroneously reporting the type of loan can also hurt. My bank reported a mortgage loan as an installment loan and, believe it or not, it dropped my credit score twenty-eight points. When they indicated their software could not distinguish between a real estate and an installment loan, I simply advised them that either they had to patch the software to handle this situation or they would have to delete the account from my profile. I backed up my advice with the FCRA. They chose to delete the account, rather than rewrite the software. In either case, I was happy because my credit score rose again. It pays to be informed!

6. Don't accept offers of a discount in exchange for a credit card.

Point to note: A small reduction in the price of a purchase, in exchange for a credit card, only benefits the merchant. It enslaves the consumer. Don't do it! Resist the temptation.

When an excessive amount of inquiries appears on your credit report, creditors may get the impression that you are looking for credit to compensate for financial difficulties. It may also appear that you will become overextended by taking on more debt than you have the ability to repay. Accepting an invitation to get a credit card in exchange for a ten-percent reduction in the purchase of items at a department store checkout is not worth the damage to your credit history. If you lack discipline in the use of credit cards, you are putting yourself in jeopardy of becoming enslaved to more debt.

7. Do make requests to increase your available credit without making hard inquiries.

Every time a hard inquiry is made for your credit score, it reflects negatively on it. If you can, ask for the limits on your current credit cards to be increased, rather than opening new ones when trying to increase the amount of your credit line versus the amount of credit used. The existing creditor will most probably make an inquiry on your report; however, this is viewed as a soft inquiry. Soft inquiries are not considered in the computation of your credit score. If you can accomplish this, you can benefit from an existing track record, whereas, with opening a new account to increase the available credit, you will not.

8. Do beware of filing bankruptcy.

There are three forms of bankruptcy: Chapter 7, Chapter 13, and Chapter 11. Of the three, Chapter 7 is the most severe.

Anyone, business or individual, has the right to file a Chapter 7. This method allows for all secured debts to be paid first from the proceeds of the sale of assets. Unsecured debts are terminated and are only paid if any money remains after secured creditors are paid. Certain aspects of the law permit unsecured debtors to claim various exemptions.

Chapter 13 is typically used by wage earners and small businesses. This delays and reduces the amount of payments to creditors over a period of time, which is known as a Chapter 13 plan, or an individual reorganization.

Chapter 11 is used by larger businesses and resembles a Chapter 13, but with more requirements. If all a debtor needs is a plan to pay off debts, then a Chapter 13 or Chapter 11 is preferable rather than a Chapter 7, particularly when trying to re-establish his or her creditworthiness.

Consumers filing for bankruptcy will be required to go through a government-approved credit counseling program prior to filing for bankruptcy protection. You may think this is the easy way out, but it is not as easy as it used to be. New bankruptcy laws are making it much more difficult to just walk away from your debts.

If you are thinking of filing bankruptcy to avoid foreclosure, don't do it! The only part of the mortgage that can be put into bankruptcy is the past due amount, the arrearage. Your mortgage payment will still be due each and every month just as before. Yes, you will have saved your home from foreclosure, but now you will have two payments: the payment for the ongoing mortgage and the payment for the bankruptcy. The ARMS (adjustable rate mortgages) will still adjust if not refinanced. In the case of a mortgage, it is better to either work out a loan modification agreement through your mortgage company's loss mitigation department or a short sale with an investor. Each can be discussed with your mortgage lender.

With a loan modification, there is a possibility that the mortgage company will attach the arrearage to the end of the note. For this consideration, your mortgage payment will adjust slightly; however, you can go forth with the new mortgage payment as the arrearage will not be due any longer. Your mortgage will no longer be in danger of foreclosure. The lender will most likely charge a fee for this service.

A short sale relieves you of the obligation to pay and simultaneously saves you from having a foreclosure reporting in your credit profile. The way it works is the mortgage company agrees to accept less than the principal balance as settlement of the debt, and the house is sold. A short sale is a long and drawn out process controlled by the lender. The lender will mandate that the home is listed for sale with a licensed realtor first for a specified number of days. The short sale will be considered only after the house does not sell.

Your bankruptcy history will stay on your credit report for a period of ten years. Therefore, bankruptcy should only be used as a very last resort.

9. Don't avoid paying your taxes.

If you think credit card companies can be nasty, the IRS and other tax collecting agencies can make them look like angels. However, you should not just ignore them. If you believe you were taxed unfairly, hire a good tax attorney, if you have the means, and fight back.

Keep in mind, also, that if you have the time and confidence, it is not necessary to hire a representative. These days, the IRS is extremely amenable— unless they detect that you are trying to avoid paying your taxes. If you can't pay your tax bills, work out a payment schedule with them even if it takes years and years to pay the bills off. Contact them before they contact you. They like to know that you are willing to work with them. Keep the lines of communication open.

A tax lien appears on your credit report as a derogatory item in the Public Section. It can remain there for seven years once it has been released for payment. If you never pay it, it can stay on your credit report indefinitely.

10. Do remember that time is of the essence.

The longer there is positive credit history reporting in your credit file, the better it is for your credit score. Establish a long history of paying your bills on time. In order to do this, you must keep credit flowing through your file. Having credit cards with zero balances will not help. One method is to charge everyday expenses on your credit cards—e.g., utility bills and gas—then have the credit companies deduct the money automatically from your checking account monthly. Be sure that the funds are deducted within the free interest period that the credit card companies provide, to avoid paying interest on the debt. Because you are paying the credit card on time every month, with this plan, you are improving your credit score by showing responsibility toward paying your bills.

It is not a good idea to close accounts with zero balances that are in good standing. If the account is a revolving credit card with a long history of good credit, closing it may lower your credit score. If you must close the account to protect against charging it up again, contact the credit reporting agency and ask that the credit history continues to report in your file. There are no guarantees.

When closing opened accounts, be sure to close the accounts with the shortest payment history, and leave open those with the longest payment history. This will lengthen the period of active credit usage in your file, which is what the credit scoring model is designed to identify. This is why it is imperative that if you close a revolving account, one with a long history of reporting positively, the history remains intact so that your score will not be penalized by the credit scoring model.

Not all of the reporting agencies report good credit beyond the seven year period. Nevertheless, it will not hurt to request that it does.

How to Increase Your Credit Score—Fast!

By now, you've requested a copy of your credit report and, possibly, you are quite dismayed at what you see. As I've mentioned, studies have shown that anywhere from twenty-five to eighty percent of reports contain errors and those are only the ones they know about. Simple things like a wrong address, an incorrect Social Security number or a mistyped credit card number can wreak havoc on your report and take you many months to correct. You could be in the situation where everything is being reflected correctly in your credit history; however, either quite a few late payments or just too much debt is causing your credit score to suffer.

Whatever the situation, you need to increase that score fast. Here are some tips to get you started:

Pay your bills on time—particularly those that are reported to the credit bureaus. These include mortgage payments, credit cards and car loans, as opposed to medical bills and utilities. We will discuss prioritizing in greater detail later.

If you are having trouble making your payments, contact your lenders right away. The worst thing you can do is ignore them. Explain your financial situation and agree on new payment schedules that you can manage.

Get the agreements in writing and ask them to include notes that your payments will not be reported as late.

If you need help working out a realistic budget and payment plan, find a low- or zero-cost agency to help you. There might be free services available from your employer, military base or credit union, or from a local branch of the U.S. Cooperative Extension or housing authority. Watch out for the sharks who want to charge you high fees for this service. We will talk more about this later.

Experts recommend paying at least the minimum amount due each month plus $10. Make sure the payment arrives at least one day before the due date. I highly recommend online bill paying which should be a free service from your bank. The day you receive the bill, you can schedule the payment, even if it is not due for another few weeks. This way, you will never forget to pay a bill, you will have written proof that the payment was made on time, and you won't have to worry about delays in the mail. Once you have all your creditors set up on the system, it will take you more time to open the envelope than it does to pay the bill. From this point, you will only have to ensure that the funds are in the bank. I use this system religiously and my payments have never arrived late.

If you have used over thirty-five percent of the current limit on your credit cards, ask for increases in your limits. Then, don't spend that extra credit! Pretend it is not real. It is only there to facilitate a quick boost in your credit score by improving your debt to available credit ratio.

Never bounce a check. If you forget to recover a check that you issued when there was not enough funds to cover it in your bank account, an NSF check, and the merchant sends that check to a collection agency, it will stay on your credit report for seven years. To avoid this, ask your bank for a small amount of reserve credit that will cover any "insufficient funds." If you are a valued customer at the bank, they should have no problem with this request.

If your bank does not have an overdraft protection system, ask your personal banker to call you if ever you overdraw your account. You will normally have until 10:00 a.m. to deposit money to cover the overdraft. This action also saves the bank money because they do not have to return the check to the merchant. Incidentally, if the bank will honor your request, they will be saving you money because the merchant will be denied the opportunity to charge you an NSF fee. Your bank may or may not charge for this service. If the bank does charge for this service, at least you will only be subjected to one fee and not two— the charge by the bank for the NSF and the charge the merchant imposes for issuing to them a bad check. Both of these charges can very well exceed sixty dollars.

As I've mentioned, recent credit history counts more than the distant past. If you do not have any open lines of credit included in your credit report for the last two years, take out a loan from your credit union or bank and open a savings account with the funds. Let the funds secure the loan; thus, you will only pay a 2% difference in interest rate on the debt. Why? The amount of interest that you pay on the debt should be no more than

2% higher than the interest that the bank pays on the money securing the loan.

Don't be tempted to use the money for anything else! Remember, you are going to become a real estate investor or purchase a home, if you do not already have one. Let this be your motivation to do the right thing.

Make this a short term loan—less than a year. If necessary, ask a friend or relative to cosign the loan. As you pay back the loan each month, the activity will be reported to the credit bureaus. Although you will be paying a higher interest rate than you are receiving from your savings account, it will still be far cheaper than paying credit card interest. This loan will force you to save money because once the loan is paid off, the money you borrowed will still be in the bank. Not only will you just have established a good credit history and created a relationship with the bank, but you will have saved money as well— and it only will have cost you two percent in interest.

Fix any errors on your credit report. Look at every item on your credit report from all three agencies. Immediately dispute *ALL erroneous* data. It is unlawful to dispute accurate information on your credit report.

Use this sample dispute letter as a guide.

Your Name
Your Address
Your City, State, Zip

Date

Complaint Department   CMMR # : [*Insert certified receipt number*]
Name of Credit Bureau   Fax Letter to [*Fax number*]
Credit Bureau's Address
Credit Bureau's City, State, Zip

Dear Sir or Madam:

I am writing to dispute the following information in my file. The items I dispute also are en-circled on the attached copy of the report I received. For identification purposes, I have en-closed a copy of my driver's license, SSN, and a utility bill *[or other document, such as bank letter with account number removed]* bearing my name and current address. In addition, the following information serves to update my personal information:

> Insert Name
> Insert Address
> Insert City and State
> Insert Employment Information (Optional)

[Repeat the following statement for each item disputed. Use as many sheets as necessary to complete dispute.]

1. *[Item disputed account number, name of item disputed, identify type of item]* I am disputing this item as *[inaccurate or incomplete]* because *[describe what is inaccurate or incomplete and why]*. I am requesting that the item be deleted *[or request another specific change]* to correct the information.

2. Item disputed account number, name of item disputed, identify type of item I am disputing this item as *[inaccurate or incomplete]* because *[describe what is inaccurate or incomplete and why]*. I am requesting that the item be deleted *[or request another specific change]* to correct the information.

3. Etc.

I have enclosed copies of documentation supporting my position. Please investigate the disputes and either delete or correct the disputed items as soon as possible.

Sincerely,

[Your Signature] _____

]Your Name Typed]

Challenge Those Mistakes

If you do find an error, you need to quickly and carefully get it corrected by issuing a dispute to all of the credit reporting agencies. Be sure to access my website, www.theroadtocreditrepair.com, for letters that can be downloaded for disputing errors and other issues on the credit report. Under the Fair Credit Reporting Act, the credit bureau must investigate any information that you believe is inaccurate within thirty days. They must contact the store, mortgage company, or bank who reported the erroneous information, who then must investigate the dispute and then report back to the credit bureau. All of this must be done within thirty days.

If the original lender agrees that the information is inaccurate, they have to notify each credit bureau so the correction to your credit profile can be made trilaterally. If the reinvestigation does not result in your favor, you can ask the credit bureau to include a statement in your file to support your case and include it with any future credit reports. This statement must be one hundred words are less. An example is provided below.

Sample of a 100 Word Explanation of Derogatory Credit

"On May 12, 1992, I became unemployed. As a consequence, the income in my household was significantly decreased, which created a financial hardship in my household, causing my inability to pay some debts. I am now employed, and as you have noticed, the delinquent payments have been brought current. The problem has been corrected, and I do not anticipate any problems in the future."

To get the process rolling, first put everything in writing. Send certified letters to the credit bureau as well as to the creditor. You can use the following example as a guide. Tell them exactly why you believe the information is incorrect and include any evidence you have such as a canceled check or other proof of payment (copies, not originals). Also when communicating with the credit reporting agency, enclose a copy of your credit report with the mistake circled. However, *do not send your credit report to the creditor.* Why? The reason that I would not send my credit report to the creditor is to protect against people having access to your entire credit history who do not have a need to know. With so much customer service being outsourced, it is hard to tell to whom or in which country your information is being processed. Take the position that it is better to be safe than sorry. The credit bureau has access to your entire credit profile anyway. The creditor does not. Only those with a need to know should have information concerning your credit. No one else!

The credit bureau does have the right to decide if a dispute is frivolous or irrelevant so don't dispute everything for the heck of it. The good news is that if any information cannot be verified, it must be deleted from your file.

After the investigation is completed, the credit bureau has to send you its written results and a free copy of your credit report, if the dispute resulted in a change. If you ask, the credit bureau must send a notice of correction to anyone who received a copy of your credit report during the past six months.

If you are in the process of applying for a mortgage or any other type of loan that you are in a hurry to receive, you can speed up the correction process by asking about a "rapid rescoring" service. An independent credit reporting company that works for the lender can help you quickly correct an error that is causing you to be rejected for a loan or forcing you to accept a higher interest rate.

To get a quick surge in your credit score, engaging in rapid rescoring is a sure bet. To use this process to your advantage, all you have to do is pay an outstanding debt and submit documentation that the debt was paid to an agency for them to update your credit profile. A mortgage broker, or other lender, can handle this for you. Once this is done, the scoring model can be invoked to calculate your score again immediately.

When debt on several accounts was settled or eliminated using this method, I have seen the credit score rise more than 50 points. There is a fee for this service and there is no guarantee of how high the score will rise.

Myths Versus Facts: Improving Your Score

Myth: Closing old accounts that you don't use much anymore will improve your score.

Fact: Your FICO score calculates the total credit you have available versus how much you have spent against that total. If you cancel all your old accounts, that will decrease the amount of credit available. Plus, lenders want to see a long credit history so you don't want to close all your old accounts. If you must close something, close some of your old department store cards but keep most of your old credit card accounts such as Visa and MasterCard.

Myth: If you find a mistake on a credit report from one bureau, they will send the corrected information to the other two.

Fact: You have to contact all three bureaus as they don't share information with each other.

Myth: If you dispute virtually all the bad stuff on your credit report, you will eventually win, whether you are in the wrong or not.

Fact: Under the Fair Credit Reporting Act, you can only dispute items that are inaccurate, misleading or unverifiable.

Myth: Credit bureaus make all the decisions about whether or not to loan you money.

Fact: The lender makes the decision based upon the information submitted by the credit bureau. The lender may also ask about your salary and employment before making a decision.

Myth: Once you make arrangements to pay an old credit card debt, your credit score will automatically improve.

Fact: Debt stays on your credit report from the date of last activity. Therefore, if an older debt is paid, particularly after it had been charged off, paying the debt extends it on the report for seven years past the date of payment. Before you pay a debt that will expire in a couple of years, ensure that in exchange for payment, the debt will be removed completely. If it is recent credit, try to get an agreement in writing from the lender, saying that they will not report the payment as late in exchange for your making full or partial payment. Just remember that the older the debt, the less attention paid to it by the credit scoring model.

Next, we are going to talk about how to handle our favorite people: BILL COLLECTORS.

CHAPTER 6

When Collectors Call

No matter how difficult the challenge,
when we spread our wings of faith
and allow the winds of God's spirit to lift us,
no obstacle is too great to overcome.

— ROY LESSIN

Have you ever had the unpleasant experience of dealing with a bill collector? I had a dispute once with someone who worked on my house. This person was one of our regular subcontractors—one that I felt I could trust. He performed work outside of the regular contract and because we had a professional working relationship, I assumed he would be charging per the going rate. Rule number one: get all work and change orders in writing, including the charges.

It wasn't that I couldn't afford to pay his charges; on the contrary, I refused to pay. As a builder and remodeler, I knew his charge was excessive for the amount of work he was performing. So I paid what I thought was fair and included a letter of explanation. Like an idiot, I didn't secure a final lien waiver before I paid him.

A lien waiver is a document that you present to the contractor to sign to protect against the contractor filing a lien against your property. Had I made him sign a notarized lien waiver, he would not have had any rights. Since I didn't, sure enough, he turned his invoice over to a collection agency and they started calling. For a copy of a lien waiver, access my website, www.theroadtocreditrepair.com. To modify the document to fit your scenario, copy and paste it into your word processor. Be sure to use it each time you pay a contractor for work performed on any of your properties. This will be your protection against corrupt contractors.

The first bill collector was really obnoxious and I refused to give him the time of day. The second was a young woman from a law firm and she was genuinely interested to hear my side of the story. She worked with me and my subcontractor and an agreement was reached. Matter closed. I settled the debt, even though I felt I was right, because my credit was more important than the couple of hundred dollars that we were fighting over. Rule number two: if you have an opportunity to prevent negative history from being entered into your credit profile, do what you can to keep your history positive.

I have many anecdotes I can share dealing with bill collectors—mine as well as my home buyers. So many that I could write a book! I am an expert in this area. You will be, too, once you understand the laws.

When I was faced with repairing the credit of some of my home buyers, I had to make contact with the bill collector to negotiate settlement of the debt and to have it removed from the credit report. Just keep in mind this: the bill collector's primary purpose is to recover the debt. "Recovering the debt" means the debtor pays it in full or settles the amount owed at a reduced amount.

Perhaps you have already had the unpleasant experience of

dealing with a debt collector. Your best protection in this case is to know your rights and what collectors can and can't do by law. If they sense any kind of hesitation or weakness, they will go for the jugular, making you miserable, as they have been trained to do.

Some of them are nice and will work with you. However, these are few and far between. They will tell you all sorts of things that may or may not be true. If you know the law, however, and deal from a position of strength, they will back down just like any schoolyard bully.

What Are Collection Agencies?

I can't imagine doing this for a living, but collection agencies really are legitimate businesses—sometimes even attorneys—who earn money by collecting old debts for creditors. I liken them to bounty hunters.

The age of the debt these collectors are looking to recover varies—usually from six months to several years past its statute of limitation. Sometimes they work on commission which can be as much as thirty to fifty percent of the money they bring in. Other times, they actually buy old debts for pennies on the dollar. Whatever they can collect above and beyond that is their profit.

Since collectors do this every day and deal with people from all walks of life, they are trained to deal with any type of response from you. This does not mean that you should feel intimidated, but rather that you should know the importance of learning your rights and what they can and cannot do. You do not have to talk to bill collector, and you do not have to be coerced into paying when the money just isn't available.

What Can They Do?

The first thing to keep in mind is that although an unpaid bill will show up on your credit report for seven years, after that time you are in the clear. States also have statutes of limitation for delinquent debts and after that time, no one can put it on the credit report; however, they can sue, as long as the time to sue is still viable. This time may vary from state to state. Collectors cannot make any threats of legal action. If they do, they are breaking the law.

Although you may feel a moral obligation to pay the bill, if you make a partial payment or in some cases even admit that you owe the money, this can restart the bill's clock on your credit report for another seven years. So be very careful about what you say over the phone once you are contacted. If someone calls you about an old debt that is beyond the statute, say little or nothing. Don't agree to pay and don't acknowledge that you might owe the money. Simply prepare to hang up the phone—but, before you do, get the collectors' contact information and send them a certified letter telling them never to contact you again. Sample letters for terminating annoying calls from debt collectors can be found on my website, www.theroad-tocreditrepair.com. For convenience, I have provided a sample letter to terminate annoying calls from debt collectors.

Sample Letter to Terminate Debt Collector's Calls

Your Name
Your Address
Your City, State, Zip

Date

Collector's Name   CMMR # : [*Insert certified receipt number*]
Collector's Business Name   Fax Letter to [*Fax number*]
Collector's Address
Collector's City, State, Zip

Re: Letter to Cease and Desist Contact in reference to [*Account Number / Creditor*]

Dear [*Collector's Name*],

Per our conversation today, I informed you that I consider your constant phone calls to be annoying and a form of harassment.

I am demanding that you no longer contact me in any manner or at any location concerning the captioned debt. According to the Fair Debt Collection Practices Act, [15 USC 1692c] Section 805(c): CEASING COMMUNICATION, you are required to cease all communication with me upon notification in writing that I do not wish to communicate with you concerning this debt. *This letter is your formal notification.*

Under the auspices of the federal FDCPA, now that you have been notified to cease contact with me, you are only allowed to contact me to deliver the following information:

1. You are planning to terminate further collection efforts;
2. You are informing me of remedies that your company normally takes to collect debts;
3. You are proceeding to take action in accordance with remedies normally taken.

Please know that I am extremely conscious of my rights. If you or your company contacts me further, you will be in violation of the FDCPA. Because you have my current address, you are prohibited, under section 805(b)2 of the FDCPA, to contact a 3rd party in reference to anything concerning the business associated with [*Account Number / Creditor*], where I am concerned.

Please know that I am accurately documenting all contact with you, inclusive of all correspondence from you and your company. Per the law, I am putting you on notice that I will be tape recording all phone calls from you or your company. If I hear from you or anyone represented by your company henceforth, I will institute all available legal actions to protect me and my family from any of your further harassment.

Sincerely,
[Your Signature]_____
]Your Name Typed]

Within the Statute of Limitations

As for newer debts that are still within the statute of limitations, a collector will first contact you to say you have an unpaid balance with a creditor. At this point, you should ask for proof that the debt is your responsibility, and that they have a legal right to collect it from you. They need to come up with a signature, a receipt, a check in your handwriting from your bank, or something else that shows this is your debt. Many times, they do not have this information since the debt has been passed around to a variety of agencies. When you ask for this proof, they must stop all collection activity until they can come up with it. This includes making any reports to the credit bureaus.

Within five days they will send you a letter stating the amount you owe, the name of the creditor, whatever proof they have, and what to do in order to pay the debt or challenge the claim. You then have thirty days to respond if you believe you do not owe this amount and they cannot contact you again.

If you do owe the money and they don't have the proof of authorization, you can tell them to stop contacting you or you will sue them under the Fair Debt Collections Practices Act. Although if they have proof, such as a copy of a sales receipt, they do have the right to keep contacting you.

However, this does not mean that you have to disclose any personal information such as where you work, how much money you have in the bank, current salary, etc. Even though they have the right to contact you, they cannot contact you at home or at work if you send them a letter ordering them to cease and desist from contacting you at those locations.

Harassment

If you feel you are being unduly harassed, send a certified letter with a return receipt requested to the collection agency and demand that they stop calling you. Legally, they cannot contact you again except to say that the creditor or collection agency will be taking some legal action. Keep a record of all letters sent and received, the name of the person who keeps calling, and detailed notes of each conversation including dates, times, language used, etc. You will need this if you plan to file an official complaint or even a lawsuit with your state attorney general.

The very best proof of harassment is a taped conversation. Thirty-five states allow you to secretly tape a telephone conversation, but if yours is not one of them, you must inform the caller in order to tape. You can simply buy a small tape recorder and put it next to a speakerphone to tape any conversation.

What Can't They Do?

In their zeal to earn a commission many collection agencies do overstep the line and become abusive. Protections were put in place by the Fair Debt Collection Practices Act of 1977 to ensure that you are treated fairly and to prohibit such activities as:

Calling before 8 a.m. or after 9 p.m.

Using threats or obscene language.

Talking to anyone else besides you or your attorney about the debt.

Threatening to garnish your wages or seize property, if this is not allowed in your state. Find out from your state's attorney general's office.

Falsely claiming to be attorneys, credit bureau representatives, law enforcement officials, or from a government agency.

Calling you at work if you have asked them not to.

Calling repeatedly and continuously to annoy and harass you.

Trying to collect more than the original debt, unless your state allows for a service charge for collections.

Claiming that they intend to sue you, unless they do plan to take legal action and are allowed to do so in your state.

Claiming that you will be arrested if you do not pay.

Sending you documents that look like official forms from a court or government agency but are not.

Depositing post-dated checks early.

What You Can Do to Report Abuses And Take Control

If you feel you have adequate proof that a collection agency has broken the law, you can sue them in a state or federal court within one year from the date of the violation. If you win, you may receive money for any damages you may have suffered, plus an additional amount up to $1,000. Court costs and attorney fees may also be recovered.

For any type of harassment that has gotten out of control, file a complaint with the attorney general's office in your state, as well as with the Federal Trade Commission. You can file your complaint with them online at http://www.ftc.gov.

How to Resolve the Matter and Get Them Off Your Back

It is always better to deal with the original creditor rather than a bill collection agency. Creditors will have to pay agencies a large percentage of the debt so they may come out ahead if they can collect even some of the money directly from you.

Call the creditor and ask to speak with a supervisor. You want a decision maker, not someone who is just going to pass along the information. On some occasions, the contract with the collection agency may prevent them from entering into negotiations with you. In this case, there is nothing that can be done about it. You will have to speak to the collection agency.

On the chance they are free to talk with you, try to work your best deal with the creditor. Tell them you would much rather work with them to ensure that the full amount of the payment gets to them. Some debt collectors cheat. Not all are honest. I have experienced situations where the money was not sent to the creditor and I had to prove that the debt was paid to the collection agency.

If your debt has already been charged off, you will have good bargaining power to work out a deal. Come up with a number you are willing to pay—say, seventy percent of the original bill. Then start by offering them forty percent and slowly come up to the seventy-percent point—kind of like haggling when buying a new car. Part of the deal must be that they remove or change the late payment notation on your credit report. They will tell you that it's impossible or illegal but, believe me, they know how to do it. The higher the debt, the more leverage you will have to work out an agreement. It will be easier to get the debt removed if working with the creditor than the collection agency. If they just downright refuse to remove the debt, ask if they will upgrade the rating.

If you do agree on a number, write up the agreement and fax it to them, requesting they sign the agreement. Ask them to fax an acknowledgement and return the original through the mail. It is mandatory that you maintain a paper trail.

Once you get an executed original of the agreement, send a certified check or money order with a notation on it saying "Payment in Full." Be sure to send your payment via certified mail and request a return receipt. This way, you know when the payment was received and who signed for it. I would not pay with a credit or debit card and do not issue a check over the phone. Doing so leaves you vulnerable for identity theft and other fraudulent abuses of credit piracy.

Push for an immediate update to your credit report. In the interim, send the executed copy of the original agreement to the credit bureaus and dispute the entry in your credit report under the status "Debt Settled/Paid in Full." When you do this, it forces the creditor to update the credit profile per the auspices of the FCRA.

If they do not respond to the credit bureaus' request for an update within the 30 day period, the debt will drop off the credit report. Moreover, by taking this action, you will not have to pay for a credit report to check whether the debt was removed because once you make the dispute, the credit bureaus will send you a copy of your report with their re-investigation results.

If by chance the debt still appears on your report when you receive it, write to the creditor demanding they live up to their signed agreement and start the dispute process over again. However, if the credit bureau does its job, this will never happen.

Point to note: you must work with the entity that reported the negative information about the debt you are resolving to the credit bureau. No other entity can remove the information or update it. Before you start negotiating, know with whom you can negotiate. If the collection agency put the debt onto the report and you negotiated a settlement with the creditor, put in your settlement offer a condition that the creditor instructs the collection agency to update the credit bureaus per the agreement.

Using Collection Agencies to Your Advantage

Believe it or not, collection agencies can play positive roles acting as middlemen in resolving old debts that are legitimate and still within the statute of limitations. If you can work out a payment plan favorable to you, this will improve your credit score and you will avoid being taken to court.

Without giving them any personal financial information, simply tell them how much you are able to pay each month. If you owe someone $1,000, for example, you could offer to pay $50 for the next twenty months. The collection agency won't be too happy, but they may go for it as $50 is better than nothing. It's tough to get water from a stone!

However, they will probably suggest borrowing from friends or family, taking out a home equity loan, or putting the debt on another credit card. This will only put you deeper into debt, so don't agree to it. And always state that part of the deal is that the creditor must remove any negative information about the debt from your credit report. In essence, this negates the negative by creating an opportunity for you to build a good credit trade line in your profile.

Collection agencies want to get money from you as quickly as possible so they will not be happy about a long-term payment plan and will try to force you to agree to their terms. Make your offer once or twice, but if they won't agree, end the conversation.

If you do happen to agree on a number, collectors will then try to get you to sign up for a payment plan that withdraws money from your checking account, using postdated checks or automatic electronic withdrawals. They will try to insist that it has to be done this way, but there is no law that says you have to comply with this request.

You want to pay by any method that does not reveal your personal bank account information. Offer to send a bank draft or money order, although these may result in additional service charges. If you agree to postdated checks or automatic withdrawals, you run the risk that the collectors will cash the checks early or more money will be withdrawn than you authorized. In any case, do not send any money until you receive a signed payment agreement from them.

One more thing, if they are collecting a debt that has not been written off by the original creditor, be sure to copy the creditor on all funds that are sent to the agency.

Student Loans

The infamous defaulting on a student loan! I have seen the failure to repay a student loan absolutely kill a credit score. Many borrowers have been blocked from obtaining a mortgage loan as a consequence of this irresponsibility. There was always a good reason for not repaying the loan (so the buyer thought). However, the lender takes the position that you were loaned the money to get an education, now it is time to pay it back. Don't despair! There is hope and a remedy for recovering from the damage done to the credit report.

If an unpaid student loan is in collection, you can apply for "reasonable and affordable payments" under the 1992 Higher Education Act. If you can prove you have a financial hardship, you can pay as little as $10 per month for at least six months. As long as you make the payments on time, you are eligible for Title IV Student Aid and can continue making these low payments until your financial condition improves.

You can also avoid collection activity by either having the loan deferred or by requesting forbearance. Deferment of a student loan allows suspension of the obligation to repay once the qualifying criteria is met. I do know that if you are a student who is enrolled in an approved academic program with at least a part-time status, you can have your loan deferred. Forbearance, on the other hand, allows for the modification of an established repayment schedule.

Before either a deferment or forbearance will be granted, the loan cannot be in default. If the loan is in default, the default status must be cured prior to obtaining a deferment or forbearance. Neither deferment nor forbearance will cancel the debt, but the repayment of the debt will be prolonged.

There are specific requirements that must be met before a loan can be deferred or forbearance can be granted. For convenience in understanding your options for repayment of a student loan, you can access a copy of the U. S. Department of Education Federal Student Aid Borrowers Services Manual from my website, www.theroadto-creditrepair.com. This is a manual that the Department of Education publishes which explains in great detail the options available for the financially-challenged borrower, parent or student, who may be experiencing difficulty paying back a student loan.

In case you are wondering how your student loan reached the grasp of the bill collector, the federal government mandates that all defaulted student loans are reported to the credit bureau and recovery of the debt made by a collection agency.

However, if you have a student loan reporting in your credit profile and you are no longer in default, you can apply to the loan rehabilitation program for relief. Once the conditions are satisfied, the negative reporting of the student loan will be deleted from your credit history.

For more information on how to take advantage of this opportunity, refer to page 19 in the U. S. Department of Education Federal Student Aid Borrowers Services Manual.

Nothing to Fear

I hope by now you are convinced that debt collectors should not be feared. By knowing and understanding the law, you can prevent harassment. By working with them to devise a payment plan for a legitimate unpaid bill, they can act as a middleman between you and the creditor. In this case, if the debt is resolved satisfactorily, you may be in a position to improve your credit.

In an abusive situation, you can demand respect or simply just hang up the telephone. If you can establish a working relationship, a deal can be cut to save you from legal actions and the negative debt can result in a positive entry recorded into your credit profile. In this situation, everyone wins in the end.

Now that we know how to handle the bill collector, let's move on and address our main goal: getting you over your debt!

CHAPTER 7

Debt: Get Over It

If we had no winter,
the spring would not be so pleasant;
if we did not sometimes taste of adversity,
prosperity would not be so welcome.

— ANNE BRADSTREET

Whenever you are having a bad day from thinking about how much debt you are in, think of how sweet freedom will taste once you finally break free. This is the light at the end of the tunnel that should be the central point of your focus.

Yet and still, I feel you! I've been there. It is so much easier said than done. It had gotten so bad in my life that I arose each morning and I wrote prayer poems before I dared to face the day. I did this every morning until I overcame the debt that kept us in bondage. To give you an idea of how long it took, I wrote nearly 300 poems in 2002.

The first housing development my husband and I built faced financial challenges because we ventured at a time when prices were tumbling in Texas. Not only that, but the venue was not the best and we had to build this development using hard money. Although it was a losing investment, we made the decision to stick with it because to walk away meant to give up—on our dreams, and on the homeowners who bought into those dreams by building their dream houses in our development.

Giving up was not an option! We could not betray those who lived there. Yes, it was bad for us, but it was not their fault. We had no choice but to stand and face adversity. It was the right thing to do—a bad business decision, but the morally correct thing to do. Besides, our only other option was bankruptcy which we did seriously consider. Had we filed bankruptcy, everyone would have lost because the development's value would have collapsed, taking down everyone associated with it. I am so very thankful that it did not come to that.

I believe that in the face of adversity, the feet and the knees are the tools that you have to intermix with action. When you plant your feet and kneel in search of spiritual guidance, a second wind blows in your favor. Mixed with a solid plan, that wind—faith, courage, and strength—wins over adversity every time.

For the first time, we developed a viable plan and performed according to it. In the end, we prevailed and it proved to be a good decision not to walk away. Although it was more difficult than we'd like to express, with an attitude change, spiritual intervention, determination, and true grit, we pulled it off.

Today, the Enchanted Villas at Woody Creek Subdivision thrives and has turned out to be the most quality-constructed housing development in the southern sector of Dallas, Texas—the only one of its kind. However, the decision to fight for it brought with it a massive amount of debt. Although it was largely business debt, it transferred to us, as we had personally guaranteed all of it—each one of those million dollars we borrowed. That, plus our existing personal debt, was a nightmare.

However, we overcame it all, saved the development, and cataloged a very valuable lesson in the process. What grew from that experience was maturity, pragmatism, and a profound feeling of accomplishment. The victory was so phenomenal that it inspired this book.

Why am I telling you this again? Because I want you to understand fully, first and foremost, that it is not going to be easy, but still you have to stick with it. Along the way to eradicating your debt, you are going to want to just say, "Forget it." Don't! The sweet taste of victory and all of the rewards that it brings—assets, money in the bank, a million net in real estate, positive recognition, clout, improved credit scores, creditworthiness, a balance sheet, the ability to play banks against each other for your business, and the ultimate feeling of accomplishment—make it worth the struggle.

During the time before I reformed, my spending habits were atrocious. For a long time, I was impressed by the wrong things. In the circle in which we were traveling, it was fashionable to be fashionable, surrounded by expensive, material things—and useless, hollow debt. You know my story: I spent money like water running from a faucet. My kids always wore the best. My youngest went to a private school. My oldest daughter thought one designer store was her personal closet and we took care of the bills. It was disgusting how we spent money. Our priorities were clearly in the wrong place.

In addition to all of this, I had my charities that I continually supported. I still do and I support them generously. The difference is, I can afford to do it now.

In making a lifestyle change, we had to distance ourselves from the root of the evil that kept us in debt. You, too, will have to identify your demons and bury them. If you don't, you won't succeed! Just as the addict has to move away from the addiction, you will have to abandon the forces that cause you to take your hard-earned money for granted.

Remember how, out of frustration, I quit my job and I vowed never to work again for someone else? I would not advise anyone else to ever do this. When you get so desperate that you quit a job that pays the kind of money I was making because you're *tired*, there is an emotional disorder that needs to be addressed. If you are at the breaking point—and you know if you are—before you do something this drastic, seek professional help. Then develop a plan of action and then, and only then, quit the job.

This is the reason why our start was so difficult. There was no real plan and the unhappiness that provoked my retreat from my job still existed. I was thinking with my emotions and not my head. What I should have done was make preparations to quit over a specified period of time, deal with the stress factors, and eliminate all of our debt first so our nest egg could have remained a nest egg. When you don't do it the right way, the odds for success are virtually nil!

If nothing else, understand this: with a change in lifestyle comes a change in spending habits. It's that simple! There is just no way around this realization. If you are going to become debt-free, improve your credit score, and start to build wealth, you *must* condition yourself to change your spending habits and start focusing on the light that is at the end of the tunnel for you—*your dreams.*

It's easy for someone else to stand back and say, "Here's where you could save money every week." Or "Buying that is really stupid." We all have to face our own spending demons and the internal forces that inspire them and figure out a plan to get ourselves out of our current debt. Then for success in the future, we must permanently mend our ways.

This has to be a decision that you make. You have to become so tired of being tired that you become consumed with creating a better lifestyle.

Though I share with you the benefits of my experience, I can only set the road for you to follow. The ultimate success is up to you to claim. As the saying goes, "You can lead a horse to water, but you can't make it drink." You are the only one who can make this success happen for you.

> *The big secret in life is that there is no big secret.*
> *Whatever your goal, you can get there*
> *if you're willing to work.*
>
> —OPRAH WINFREY

Improving Your Credit Score Does Not Lower Your Debt

Hopefully by now, you have resolved to take some of my advice from previous chapters and are making good progress toward improving your credit score. You plan to order a copy of your report and correct any errors. You will make every effort to not spend over thirty-five percent of your credit card limit. You vow to make sure all bills are paid on time.

However, unless you are paying off old bills, improving your credit score does not automatically lower your debt! You need to figure out what you owe and what money you have coming in and then set up a payment schedule to list how you are going to pay down your debt. We will talk more about this in Chapter 10. In the meantime, the best thing you can do to lower your debt is quit adding to it!

My Philosophy of Debt

Since the time I hit bottom and successfully fought my way back to financial stability, I have developed my own personal philosophy to help control my spending. Basically, I divide all expenditures into two categories: hollow debt and empowering assets.

Hollow debt is money spent on those things we can live without if we must—those things that won't build wealth for the future. In other words, they won't "fertilize your money tree." This includes expensive vacations, dining out, the latest in electronics, fancy cars, etc.

Empowering assets are investments that will fertilize and grow your money tree such as fixing up your house, investing in new properties, or taking courses to expand your knowledge about a particular subject and later using that knowledge to start a home-based business. This is how I got my lifestyle out of hollow debt: I started to fertilize my money tree through real estate investments and multiple streams of income.

Basically, every time I have the urge to spend, I ask myself, "Will this purchase earn me money, or will it just make me feel good?" Most of the time, if the answer is not "it will earn me money," I don't buy it. Sometimes I still buy it, but you'd better believe that it's an offer that I just cannot refuse—for example, a Christmas present I've come across in July that is an excellent deal.

Honestly, the way I avoid this situation is I just shop less. When you're changing your lifestyle, you have to make lifestyle changes. There will be some hollow debt that must be purchased—food, clothes, gas, supplies—but these are daily necessities. They don't count unless you overindulge.

While going through this transformation, as a reward, I set aside shopping points and I saved them. When I do go shopping, I spend these points. How do shopping points work? You set aside a designated amount of money as a savings from funds that you don't need. I call these bucks "Feel Good Money!" This is extra money set aside specifically to satisfy the need to shop.

At the end of the month, or whenever I get a chance, I go on a shopping spree using cash instead of credit. I take my husband with me because I know he hates shopping and the stay will be short. With "Feel Good Money," I can buy whatever I want, but when the cash is gone, I'm done. I used to liken it to withdrawals because it provided a "quick fix."

Bargains are the only thing I buy. I love bragging about a great deal that I only spent $10 to obtain. I love to give gifts, too, so I buy bargains, stash them away, and when the time comes, I give them away. It is a function of my personality, except that now I don't carry the debt.

Know Why You Spend

The first step toward controlling your own spending is to sit yourself down, figure out where all your money is going and how you got into this situation in the first place. I gave you my reasons for overspending; now you need to find yours. Once you figure this out you will be well on your way to controlling your expenditures and making plans to pay off what you've already spent.

Here are just a few examples of why people overspend that I've seen over the years:

> **Deprived childhood:** Many people grew up poor and had few, if any, luxuries. Now that they have more money coming in, they feel the need to make up for lost time. Or perhaps they fear that if they don't spend it, someone will take it away.

> **Keeping up with the Joneses:** Guilty as charged! If you live in a nice neighborhood or happen to have a very successful circle of friends, you feel the need to have what everyone else does. The truth is, they are probably feeling the same way.

Emotional issues: Sometimes we joke about being "shopaholics," but this can become a very serious mental health issue just like alcoholism or gambling. Many times people shop because they are depressed, anxious, or lonely, particularly around the holiday season. They believe that if they go shopping, they will feel better when, actually, they will only feel worse. If you think you may fall into this category, visit my website, www.theroadtocreditrepair.com, to find resources to help you.

A feeling of power and prestige: If you wear expensive clothes, drive a fancy car, and eat in high-priced restaurants, it gives you the feeling that you have really "made it," and everyone else will know it. This is not a good reason to spend money if you really can't afford it. Look for other ways to get a sense of accomplishment such as in your career or by doing volunteer work.

Immediate gratification or can't say no: Many of us are the type of people who see something we like and just have to buy it without any thought as to how we are going to pay for it. We have the inability to say "No!" to a child or spouse. In a way, we become the child if we can't control our spending and stick to a budget.

Maintaining what you had: If you used to have a high income or maybe grew up rich, it is hard to change your lifestyle and spending habits if your financial condition changes. You insist on keeping up your old ways even if it leads to being overextended with a bad credit score. I, too, was guilty of this because when my lifestyle changed, my spending habits did not.

"Their" money versus mine: It's so much easier to use a credit card than cash or checks because it feels more like "their" money than yours. For some people, only using cash and just enough credit to establish a history is the best solution to avoid overspending.

Wasteful Spending

I'll bet anything that you can find something on the following list that you spend money on regularly. Most of us would agree that these are wasteful items but you may not agree that all of them are unnecessary. We all have our favorite things to spend money on which is fine—just keep in mind that you will need to make a trade-off in order to keep to the budget you will be making each week. More about that later.

Ten Examples of Wasteful Spending

Cigarettes. Need I say more? Since I've never smoked, it's easy for me to ask, "Why not quit?" If you're not going to quit for health reasons, do it for the money you will save. Five dollars a pack times 365 days a year equals a whopping $1,825. Can't you think of a better way to use that money?

Daily lattes or other fancy coffee drinks. It's so relaxing to go to one of the local coffee shops and the drinks they make are so good. But at $4 or more a cup, that adds up quickly. Get yourself a good coffee machine for home and a nice travel mug and you will save at least $1460 per year if you are a once-a-day fancy-coffee drinker.

Buying new dressy clothes for kids. How often do they wear them—once or twice per year? Children's consignment stores are full of dresses, jackets and ties at great prices. While you are there sell some clothes your child has grown out of. And if you shop in wealthy towns, you may just find a few things for yourself that are of great quality and priced low.

Toys. In the same vein, don't go out and spend a fortune on kids' toys. Shop at yard sales. You will be amazed at what you can find second-hand but in very good condition.

Pocket change. What is it about men and the change they collect in their pockets? They bring it home and throw it on the bar or keep it in a jar at work and never spend it. I can live for days on the change my husband leaves around and then I don't have to go to the ATM machine as often.

Lunches out. This is a hard one as I am one of those people who hates to pack a lunch. However, if you do this, you will save a lot of money. Try to limit yourself to a once-a-week lunch out and then it will seem like a special treat. To compensate for my eating out so much, I order from the children's menu.

Dinners out. Take-out and prepared foods at the grocery store apply here, too. This is probably the main area where most Americans waste money. You can get the same ambience in your own house with candles, a tablecloth and your good dishes as you can in a nice restaurant. If you only go out to eat once a week or less, it will seem like a very special occasion.

Trading in your car every few years. You've probably all heard that you lose up to thirty percent of a new car's value the minute you drive it out of the dealer's lot. If you don't want to buy used cars because you fear they will require more repairs than a new car, at least drive the new one "into the ground" and keep it as long as possible. This is what we do as I personally do not believe in buying used cars. Rather, we buy new cars, keep them well maintained, and drive them for ten years or more. Moreover, when we buy new, we never finance a car for more than thirty-six months and we pay them off in eighteen.

Car wash. Unless it's the dead of winter, why not wash your car in your own driveway and get the kids involved?

Gardening. If you are a gardener, instead of ordering plants from expensive catalogs or paying top dollar at the local nursery, buy them from plant sales in your town. They will be cheaper and you will know that they will grow in your area. And until you get yourself out of debt, ditch the expensive lawn service and do it yourself. It's good exercise!

Getting a New Mindset

It's really true that if you think about the pennies, they will eventually turn into dollars. How often do we throw food out because we don't want to deal with the leftovers or throw out toothpaste or laundry detergent because it's too much trouble to squeeze out the last drops?

I'm challenging you to adopt an entirely new mindset. Every waking hour try to think about how you can save money and generate additional revenue. Question every purchase you make and consider where or how you can get it cheaper.

Better yet, ask yourself if you can live without it and whether it is hollow debt or an empowering asset. In Chapter 10 we will talk in more detail about easy ways to earn additional money if you aren't doing so well on cutting expenses and paying off old debts. Having multiple streams of income will act as a catalyst to achieving your goals.

If you adopt a whole new mindset and get the entire family involved, you will be surprised at how successful you can be. Be sure to read Chapter 10 where I introduce a way to make extra income that the entire family can become involved in and it's fun.

Get a Firm Hold—Make a List

In preparation for the act of reducing your debt, which we will begin in Chapter Eight when I introduce you to my IPO Strategy, it is time to face the music and list all your debts, including the full balance of all credit cards. You will need this information to complete the IPO chart. Then, in Chapter Nine, I will introduce you to budgeting. In the interim, let's take a look at your monthly expenditures.

Make twelve columns on a sheet of paper or use an Excel spreadsheet to list all your expenses by month—such as utilities, food, gas, mortgage, insurance, car payments, etc. Look in your checkbook to get the exact amounts from past payments. (You ARE recording all your payments made by check and online, aren't you?) Why? To get a handle on your debt, you must know how you are spending your money each month.

For all payments that are not made monthly, as in insurance, compute the annual payment, then divide it by twelve to get the monthly payment. Then add up the total expenditures and subtract it from your monthly income at the bottom of the list. Hopefully, there will be some money left over at the end of the month. This is commonly referred to as a monthly cash flow statement or a monthly budget. A sample for you to use in tracking your monthly expenses can be accessed from my website, www.theroadtocreditrepair.com.

Monthly Budget Reconciliation

	Jan	Feb	Mar	Apr	May	Jun	Jul	Aug	Sep	Oct	Nov	Dec
Income												
Cash Take Home	6000											
Expenses												
Tithes	600											
Misc (Clothing, Entertainment, Dining Out, etc.)	1200											
Mortgage	1200											
Groceries	400											
Water	65											
Gas	45											
Electricity	250											
Phone	65											
Cable	65											
Cell	50											
Insurance	120											
Auto Insurance	150											
Fuel	300											
Visa	150											
Mast Card	150											
Furniture	75											
Car Note	500											
Child care	400											
Lawn Care	100											
Savings	80											
Total Expenses	5765	0	0	0	0	0	0	0	0	0	0	0
Net Income	35	0	0	0	0	0	0	0	0	0	0	0

Is there anything left over? If so, this will be the amount you can afford to use to pay off your debt each month. If not, you need to think of ways to generate some additional income. I will be giving you lots of ideas later.

What Is In Your Control?

The next step is to look at your monthly expenditures list and decide what is in your control and what is not. Hopefully, you have been honest and have included what you spend on groceries, clothing, and entertainment.

For some people, keeping an expense diary and writing down every penny they spend for a couple of weeks helps them keep track of where their money is going. You may not have the time to do this, but make time to complete the chart once a month. If you are married, get your spouse involved. Coming up with a plan to eliminate debt promotes bonding. You will become closer as you see the debt subsiding and as you toy with ideas about how to spend all your new free time, which comes from being debt-free.

Certain expenses may appear to be beyond your control such as rent or mortgage, utilities, and even medical bills. However, if you can reduce the amount of money spent on things that are under your control (eating out, expensive clothes, etc.), you can free up some cash to pay off your long-term debt.

This doesn't mean you don't have any control over your fixed costs. Here are some ideas about where you can save money on those as well:

> Lower your thermostat in the winter and raise it in the summer to save on heating and air conditioning.

> If possible, refinance your mortgage or car loan when rates go down. However, be sure to do the math and do not forget to include the refinance fees and closing costs. The goal is to save money.

> Take shorter showers and don't water your grass as often.

> Never leave a room with the lights on and train your kids to do this as well.

> Replace all of your light bulbs with fluorescent lighting.

> Make it a do-it-yourself project to make your home more energy-efficient.

Reduce the number of times per week you run the dishwasher and other appliances.

Shop around for lower insurance rates for your car and home.

Clip grocery store coupons but only those you really use or you will end up spending even more money.

Make sure you have at least the minimal health insurance for hospitalization. A car accident or unexpected illness can wipe out your savings instantly. If you can't afford it, most states have programs to assist.

Don't take out cash advances from a credit card. The interest rate ends up being about twenty-five to thirty percent, since interest accumulates from day one, unlike a credit card where you get a one-month grace period.

Don't leave too much money in your checking account. Only put in a little more than what you will need for monthly expenses and put the rest in a savings or money market account right away. You will not earn interest on money in a checking account unless you fall for a bank promotion that makes you keep $1,000 or more in the account at all times. Make your money work for you, not them.

Don't pay your bills early just because you "hate looking at them" or because you're afraid you'll forget. Cash flow is the name of the game. If you pay your bills electronically, you can set them up to be paid at a later date. If you pay by check and it arrives well before the due date, you are missing out on earning interest in your savings account.

Handle Your Debt on Your Own or Call for Help

Some of us have a lot of self-discipline and others do not. You may be in so deep you can't see the way out. Or you know you won't be able to pay off your debts any time in the near future.

There's no shame in asking for help and, as I have mentioned, there are many agencies out there that offer credit counseling services for little or no cost. Your bank or credit union may offer this or other non-profit agencies. In Chapter 11 we will be talking about what to look for when choosing a credit counseling service as there are some disreputable ones out there that will be of little help and will charge you a lot of money. In the process, they won't take care to protect your credit score from slipping further and that's the last thing you need!

In the next chapter, I would like to introduce you to my IPO strategy, which can be used to organize debt reduction. It is an effective way to see clearly your debt and to develop a plan for its elimination.

CHAPTER 8

Introduction of My IPO Strategy for Organizing Debt Reduction

There are two ways of meeting difficulties:
either alter the difficulties,
or alter yourself to meet them.

— PHYLLIS BOTTOME

Have you ever been told that you needed an attitude adjustment? Maybe whoever told you that was responding to a sad story that you were telling in which you were feeling really sorry for yourself. You were so full of "oh, pity me!" that you could not see that you were your own worst enemy. Well, that individual may have given you some excellent advice.

Oftentimes we are so close to a situation that we cannot see how we stifle our own progress. If you read the story of how my husband and I fell into debt, it is clear who was the culprit of the disaster. Our

131

irresponsibility was crystal clear to me as I was writing the story. However, until the same things kept happening time after time, I couldn't see it. After we had gone through an attitude transformation, it was easy to see, in hindsight, that we were the victims of a quagmire that only we had created.

At the time we were in denial and it was definitely someone else's fault. Oh, don't misunderstand what I am saying: The hard-money lender was trying to steal our property. This was real and truthful; however, we were at his door because of our poor creditworthiness. Otherwise, he would not have known us.

At any rate, it was only when things just kept going wrong, predicament after predicament, and we were about to lose everything, that we took a closer look at the roles we played in our fate. Sure, the hard-money lender tried to take advantage of us; however, our lifestyle enabled us to be in the position to be used. We were the only ones that could take one-hundred-percent, full responsibility for the drama that crept into our life. As the "no's" kept banging our heads against the wall, the only possible solution was to prepare to defeat the enemy or to give up. To not give up meant taking a good look at the situation, analyzing the circumstances—including our role in it—and developing a viable plan and resolution.

In his book, *Attitude Is Everything*, Keith Harrell writes that "a positive attitude is the first and last line of defense." It is easy to mix confidence with having a positive attitude. We had plenty of confidence but we were out of touch with reality and, as such, our attitude was completely skewed.

Too much money was flowing through our hands for us to have been so cavalier. Once we began to put it all into perspective, focus on the reality, develop a positive attitude, and take responsibility for the roles we played in our troubles, we began to understand that we had the POWER to make our dream come true. We had the POWER and it was within us all the time.

Our POWER came in the form of recognizing our weaknesses and putting our strengths to work to change our situation—or better yet, to empower our situation. From this change grew a more positive, more intense attitude and a desire to succeed. We had to bring order to the madness. With that altered attitude, I implemented an IPO philosophy as our defense to saving our dream. Only then did the end transform into a beginning.

The IPO Philosophy: Bringing Order to the Madness

The man who can drive himself further once the effort gets painful is the man who will win.

—ROGER BANNISTER

The gem cannot be polished without friction, nor man perfected without trials.

— OLD CHINESE PROVERB

Don't give up! Fight not for yourself, but for all who fought so that there could be a better day. Fight for those who were in your same situation, but who did not have the mentality to figure it out. If you cannot do it for yourself, do it for them; do it for those who will come behind you.

— MY AUNT, FRANCES REDDIX

We were on a mission, first and foremost, to save our development and the dream of those people who had built their dream houses in our subdivision. We were in way over our heads. If the hard-money lender could not be blocked, I knew he would destroy the flavor and integrity of the subdivision. He would either sell off the lots or build a product of much less quality.

In either case, the value of the development and the homes already standing would be severely lessened. I couldn't let that happen. We couldn't let that happen. We needed another plan—one that would work this time. If we were to survive, it would be up to us. No one else could help us. As the cliché goes, when you make your bed hard, you've got to lie in it. Our plan had to be rock solid if we were to win.

The Plan

We had less than ten months to pay the hard-money lender a million dollars. The challenge date was October 10, 2002. On October 11, either the development, our dreams, and our goals would be ours to complete or his to destroy. Ten months was all we had to find the funding and build enough houses to get him his money. Ten months to eliminate a million dollars in debt. Ten months seems like a long time but when you're standing on sinking sand, it can be very easily equated to a minute.

When I was a software engineer, we designed projects per an IPO methodology. In the financial world, an "initial public offering" is referred to as an IPO, the acronym associated with a private company going public. In the world of computers, it means Input—Process—Output and it is the methodology by which computer programs process data.

The theory centers around the premise that in order to execute the procedure to produce the desired output, you must first have the inputs clearly defined and available. The output is achieved over phases; one begins once the previous completes. Thus, you cannot start to execute the process until the inputs are identified and gathered.

In some cases, the inputs have to be generated after the process has started. If this ever occurs, the input would have to be obtained before the processing could continue.

With an IPO, a project is defined on paper with complete clarity, laying out the game plan in writing based on the three phases. This is what we needed—clarity.

I've read how, when in difficulty, a person will pull from their roots. Though I vowed never to re-enter the workforce, I was very happy to pull from my training and even more grateful that I could. Using the IPO theory brought logic to an illogical situation. Once I defined the situation, a plan grew and we were able to alleviate the debt in a ten-month timeframe.

I identified and separated the repayment of the debt into components: INPUT, PROCESS, and OUTPUT. In my head, I talked out the strategy. Then, under the respective columns, I placed my thoughts on paper where I could see clearly what was needed to bring about the result we needed.

Before I could implement the process of paying down the debt, I had to know what resources I had and what was needed to accomplish the goal. This went under the INPUT column, inclusive of the total debt. Once I had this defined, I could formulate the plan (process). I knew what the output was all too well. If you can ever get into the habit of thinking in this manner, you become an instant problem solver and any task can be accomplished with the right attitude, patience, and tenacity.

This is literally how I did it—how I improved our credit score and turned our debt into a positive net. First, I applied this principal to release us from the grasp of the devil—the hard-money lender. Then I used it to break free from the shackles of our other debt. Now we only carry what I term "good debt"—that which fertilizes our money tree.

The Procedure

First and foremost, I made a list of all our assets that I could put to work for us, both tangible and intangible:

1. The equity in the two houses: model, $300,000, and homestead, $400,000
2. The lots in the development
3. A bank account with savings to cover ten interest payments and ten house notes
4. The SUV and the pickup
5. The newspaper article
6. Contracts to purchase the homes under construction with funding stopped
7. Extra work pending
8. Promises to participate
9. Our reputation
10. Desire
11. Attitude adjustment

Notice that under assets I included reputation, desire, and attitude adjustment. This is not being a braggart. This is using all you can to strengthen your chances to succeed. If I needed to go looking for money again, we would need assets. Albeit intangible, our reputation, credentials, experience, and positive attitude were the only assets that we could offer a potential investor. Hence, accolades and amenities are assets that are extremely valid INPUTS. In addition, we had real estate that we could leverage.

Next, I made a list of all of the debt:

$750,000: the hard-money lender

$175,000: subcontractors and suppliers for stopped construction

$400,000: complete construction underway

$ 38,000: friends and family

Finally, I built an IPO scenario to organize the task of alleviating the debt.

The IPO Scenario for Saving the Subdivision

Input	*Process*	*Output*
Ascertain the Net Assets	*Formulate the Plan*	*Envision the Goal*
Inputs	Use money in bank to keep interest payments current to hard-money lender.	Eliminate $1.325 million in debt.
The house with more than $400,000 in equity and the model house worth $300,000.	Use money in bank to pay mortgage on house w/equity.	Finish the homes under construction.
The lots in the development.	Close first home in subdivision, and pay down loan by $208,000.	Pay off the hard-money lender.
A bank account with savings to cover interest payments.		Pay off friends who loaned money.
The SUV and the pickup	Use contracts to acquire financing in name of home-buyer. These are mechanics lien contracts and will provide cash flow. Pay down $272,000 to hard-money lender.	Pay the banker.
The newspaper article.		Save the development.
Contracts to purchase the homes under construction and to build via Mechanic lien contracts.	Build two spec homes using interim from friend who owns the bank. Pay $180,000 to hard-money lender.	Preserve the dreams of the existing homeowners.
Promises to participate.		Obtain clear title on model house.
Extra work pending.	(Hard-money lender paid until last balloon payment of $90,000 in October. Now, concentrate on other debt. Borrow against lots to pay balloon.)	Become creditworthy.
Our reputation, desire, and positive attitude	Refinance equity in personal real estate ($136,000) and complete four build jobs for city (CDBG) work. Pay suppliers and subcontractors $400,000 to finish the four houses where construction funding stopped. Use the proceeds to pay off $175,000 to suppliers and subs.	Improve credit scores.
		Create wealth.
Debts to be paid:		
750,000 hard-money lender		
400,000 to complete construction		
175,000 to suppliers/subs	Leverage equity in three lots to make final $90,000 payment to lender.	
38,000 to friends and family		

Notice that the OUTPUT column included what we were trying to accomplish—the goal. Our goal was to eliminate the entire $1.325-million debt, finish the homes under construction, save the development, preserve the dreams of the existing homeowners, obtain clear title on the model house, and improve our credit scores so that we could become creditworthy and begin to create wealth. Since the model house was built with funds from the hard-money lender, the title was not clear. However once his debt was paid, the model house, which appraised for $300,000, would have a clear title automatically.

Always start by defining the goal completely. The OUTPUT is the complete picture of the goal that you will be accomplishing.

Before you can begin to devise the strategy for accomplishing the goal, you must first know what you are up against. Under the INPUT column, list all of your assets—all income, money in the bank, anything that can be sold, skills, accolades that may be used to sell your abilities and boost your confidence, and all possibilities to generate income. In our case, there was real estate with equity, a very small amount of money in the bank, contracts that could be leveraged, newspaper articles that might be used to entice a partnership, contracts pending, as well as the ability to perform extra work, a promise to participate, a positive attitude, and a burning desire to succeed. Also, under the Input column, list the debt—the entire debt. You must know what you are working against in order to bring success.

Once the INPUT column is complete—that is, once the assets and the liabilities are honestly disclosed—you can start planning the procedure for eliminating the debt. This procedure is referred to as the PROCESS. Through writing out on paper the steps to eliminate the debt, you become intimately familiar with the task ahead. The steps that you will follow are written out, one by one. When all of the steps in the PROCESS are successfully performed, the OUTPUT should automatically be achieved.

The time that it takes to finish is really not that important. In our case ten months was it. We had no other choice. Either we would finish it in ten months or we would lose everything that we had. Your case may be different. Set your pace based on the amount of money you have to pay off the debt. If you want to pay it off quickly, you will have to earn more income.

Because you have itemized your assets and your liabilities, you now have a better picture of what needs to be done to eliminate the debt. In our case, our assets pretty much balanced the debt, but it was in the form of equity, which is not cash. And we needed the ability to generate cash. Though we had some cash, it was reserved to pay the interest. So for us, the cash was not useable because if we could not make the interest payments, it was over.

This is another point: If we did not have to use the cash for interest payments, we still could not put it to work for us because we lacked both the credit score and the credentials to walk into a traditional lender and apply for a loan against the equity. Normally, if you have one of the three, you can get a loan. However, it wouldn't work in our case because the amount of money needed was so large. The small amount we had in the bank would not even cover the "skin" the bank would have required as a down payment. Thus we had to work to generate the cash to pay the hard-money lender.

The method we used to generate the cash was to build houses and then sell them. If we could stick to the plan we could achieve the output. I am happy to report that we stuck to the plan and raised the money to pay off all of the debts using the assets that we listed in the INPUT column.

If you read about how we eliminated the debt, you will learn that even though we raised the money, trouble still reared its ugly head before we could claim victory. Adversity is like that—it raises challenges when we least expect it. However, because we had gone through an attitude adjustment and adopted an IPO philosophy for resolving problems, we were able to respond promptly with precision, and not just react, to sidestep the obstacles ahead that blocked our progress. We were able to strategically attack the problems that surfaced because we had a plan, a positive attitude, and transformed thinking. We were on the road to credit repair and to building wealth.

In the next chapter I will introduce the concept of budgeting. Chapter 9 will walk you through a tried and proven IPO scenario for reducing debt. It will also depict a budget to manage income after debt is eliminated. Later you will be introduced to the snowball method of debt reduction. This subject will be covered in more detail in Chapter 10.

You are doing great so far. Continue to stick with me. You almost have everything that you need to get out of debt, stay out of debt, and transform your habits into those that generate wealth.

CHAPTER 9

IPOs and a Budget— Two Important Strategies for Debt Reduction

A Case Study

*There are costs and risks to a program of action,
but they are far less than the long-range risks
and costs of comfortable inaction.*

— JOHN F. KENNEDY

Your ultimate goal is to have only "good debt"—that which fertilizes the money tree—reporting in your credit file and present on your balance sheet. If you don't have a balance sheet now, don't dismay! By the time you get your credit straight and your score improved, you'll be in a position to start turning your debt into a positive net. You will have assets and a financial statement that reflects them. Because I believe in your success, you can access a sample financial statement from my website, www.theroadtocreditrepair.com. In addition, if you have Microsoft Excel, you can modify the statement to mimic your financial picture.

In the next chapter, we will discuss how you can take charge in eliminating debt on your own. However, before I take you there, I want you to step through an actual IPO that was used to raise the credit score of one of my clients and eliminated their debt in less than 120 days.

In this example my clients had the wherewithal; however, they lacked the discipline to control their finances. Thus their credit was sloppy and they had no plan for saving money.

I had a home under construction that they were interested in purchasing. We were about 120 days away from completion. At the time when they introduced themselves to my company, they could not afford the house. Oh, they made the money, but because of their debt structure, they could not afford to pay another debt.

I knew I had 120 days to get them ready for homeownership, and with no other buyers calling, I decided to take a shot at improving both their scores and their financial situation. At the time, they were nearly $171,000 in debt with past-due payments in the amount of $30,000. Their payments each month topped $2,500 and this did not include daycare and the ordinary cost-of-living expenses such as groceries, gas, and utilities.

For brevity, I'm going to let you in on the ending now: We made it! We made it well within the timeframe needed. This case was not a difficult one because the money was available. Missing was the discipline and an IPO.

This is how we accomplished the goal. I started with a tri-merged credit report. You can pull your own online using the methods previously discussed. I obtained a copy from a mortgage broker because I wanted to have accurate credit score, at least the ones that the lenders accepted. I provide access to a sample of this type of credit report from my website, www.theroadtocreditrepair.com. I suggest that you gain experience reading this type of a credit report. When you begin to purchase real estate this is the type of credit report that the mortgage lenders use.

There were two reasons that we needed to have the credit report: One, it gave a snapshot of the credit score and debt situation and two, if the debt was not being reported by any of the agencies, we were not concerned with it at the time. We only considered utilities, child care, groceries, gas, etc. in the budget; otherwise, we did not consider it as debt.

The mission was to raise the couple's credit scores which were hovering around the high 400s, to above 620—the score needed to qualify for a mortgage—and to establish a plan for my clients to start building wealth. We used the credit report to identify the debt and the credit score. Then we listed all of the assets that could be put to work, both tangible and intangible.

1. Two jobs with a total gross income of $7500 monthly— $750 and $2250 take home pay on opposite weeks.

2. Plentiful overtime for one of the spouses—$600 per pay period.

3. A bank account with savings in the amount of $1000.

4. A home, but no equity; however, the note was only $670.

5. An SUV, a pickup, a lawn mower, a piano, a drum set, and a construction trailer.

6. A burning desire to upgrade to a larger home.

7. A teenage son.

Notice that under assets I included their burning desire to upgrade their home to a larger one and the fact that they had a teenage son. The desire to upgrade was the motivating factor and the catalyst for a speedy achievement of the goal. The teenage son could get a job to support his wants while his parents focused on his needs.

Also, the combined household net income was $6000 monthly. Because their pay periods were opposite each other, there was always cash flow. The debt could be broken into periods. Since overtime was plentiful, the husband agreed to work overtime for four months.

Next, I made a list of all of their debt that was reporting to the credit bureau:

Mortgage	$80,000	($700)
Car 1	$36,000	($687)
Car 2	$25,000	($546)
Student loans	$8,000	($100)
Installment	$8,000	($272)
Installment	$490	($23)
Installment	$467	($25)
Visa	$1,400	($89)
MasterCard	$536	($46)
Visa	$1,890	collection
Medical	$9,000	collection
Medical	$1,500	collection
Medical	$723	collection
Medical	$478	collection
Medical	$242	collection
Medical	$153	collection
Medical	$137	collection
Medical	$115	collection
Medical	$105	collection
Medical	$104	collection
Medical	$84	collection
Medical	$15	collection
Utility	$108	collection
Utility	$232	collection

The IPO Scenario for Cleaning the Credit of a Prospective Homebuyer

Input	*Process*	*Output*
Ascertain the Net Assets Inputs	***Formulate the Plan***	***Envision the Goal***
The house with no equity. Two jobs, with a total net income of $6000 monthly—$750 weekly and $2250 biweekly.	Structure debt elimination to be complete in 120 days.	Living in a brand-new, three-story home comfortably.
A bank account with savings in the amount of $1000.	Use the savings to pay the note for Car 1, to pay the utilities, and to stock up on groceries and personal items for one month. Eating out and entertainment will be suspended for the first month. Gas will be conserved by carpooling.	Only have one car note to pay. Bring the student loan current, and pay it well for six months, so the negative history can be deleted from the credit report.
An SUV, a pickup, a lawn mower, a keyboard, a drum set, and a construction trailer.		
A burning desire to upgrade to a larger home.	Contact medical facility to settle debt. The goal is to get them to accept twenty-five cents on a dollar. This will cost $3,164. $9,492 will be saved.	Ultimate goal to have only house note for the new house as debt. Be in a position to pay cash for new furniture.
A teenage son.		
	Contact collection agency to settle Visa debt in collection. Goal is to pay $945, to eliminate the $1895 debt.	Raise the credit score to over 620.

Debts to Be Paid		
Mortgage	$80,000	($700)
Car 1	$36,000	($687)
Car 2	$25,000	($546)
Student loans	$8,000	($100)
Installment	$8,000	($272)
Installment	$490	($23)
Installment	$467	($25)
Visa	$1,400	($89)
MasterCard	$536	($46)
Visa	$1,890	collection
Medical	$9,000	collection
Medical	$1,500	collection
Medical	$723	collection
Medical	$478	collection
Medical	$242	collection
Medical	$153	collection
Medical	$137	collection
Medical	$115	collection
Medical	$105	collection
Medical	$104	collection
Medical	$84	collection
Medical	$15	collection
Utility	$108	collection
Utility	$232	collection

Process (continued):

Send verification letters to credit bureau disputing debt as outstanding, once paid.

Sell the house.

Exchange the older Car 2 for a car from a relative, to eliminate the payment. ***

Pay off $490 installment debt.

Pay off $467 installment debt.

Pay off utility collection.

Pay down good Visa to $420.

Pay down MasterCard to $161.

Eliminate installment loans.

Eliminate student loan delinquency.

Accelerate payoff of Car 1.

Tithe: contribute to the church and perform community service hours a week to constitute ten percent, whenever possible.

Output (continued):

Be in a position to save twenty percent of salary monthly.

Tithe ten percent per pay period.

*** *Caution: When swapping a car or house that does not have a clear title, without completing a sale first, understand that if the person does not pay the note, you may be placing your credit in danger. If you must become involved in this type of situation, know the party with whom you are dealing and control making payments to the lender to preserve your credit score.*

Getting Started

Using the guidelines for developing an IPO from Chapter 8, I built an IPO strategy to organize the task of eliminating the debt. We first listed the goals under the Output column. The ultimate goals were to personify the desire to live in a brand-new home, to eventually pay off the second car so that they could live comfortably in this new home, to be in a position to buy new furniture, to tithe ten percent, and to save twenty percent of their salary. Per the amount of money that flowed into the home, it would be easy to accomplish the goals. I completed the Input column by listing all of the money coming in to the home and the debt that was reflected on the credit report.

Under the Process column, we wrote out the plan to eliminate the debt. The elimination of the debt was timed to be completed by the time the home was completed and we began the payment process during the week that my clients brought home $2,250.

The First Week

The first thing I did was have my clients list the house for sale and contact the medical facilities to get them to accept a reduction in the amount that was owed. Oftentimes medical facilities will accept pennies on a dollar as payment for outstanding debts. The key is to try to settle the debt with the business office of the medical provider, rather than the collection agency.

The total amount of debt owed in medical bills exceeded $12,000. The plan was to offer twenty-five percent of the debt as settlement. If the facilities accepted this amount, the debt would be paid in full. However, the facility would not be contacted and offered a settlement until the money was available, as it is rare that a settlement payment will be honored with a payment plan.

During the first week that the debt elimination began, all but the medical bills over $1,000 were settled. The total settlement amount was $539. During this same week, we settled the Visa card in collection for fifty cents on the dollar for a total of $945. From this week's pay, $766 was left for gas, groceries, miscellaneous purchases, etc.

To start saving again, $389 was placed in the savings account and $225 went to tithes. The remainder, $102, was used for living expenses during the next week.

The Second Week

During the second week, we did not pay any medical bills. The two larger ones were left and they were not as old as the others. We would wait at least a month before we would attempt to settle those debts to allow some aging of the debt to occur.

Currently there was no incentive for the provider to settle the debt and the debts were still with the collection agencies. Hopefully, based on the date indicated on the credit report, the contract with the collection agency would have expired and the debt would be returned to the provider.

So instead, I attempted to settle the utility debts for fifty cents on the dollar; however, they would only discount the debt twenty-five percent. I took the counter offer and paid off the debt.

During this week, my clients brought home $1,000. The husband earned an additional $250 for overtime worked. With this money, in addition to the utility bills, we paid off the smaller of the two installment loans. The total amount spent to cure the debt this week was $722 which left them $278. Of this money, $100 went into savings and $100 went to tithes. For the week, only $78 remained. To make ends meet, my clients brown-bagged lunch and carpooled to work.

The Third Week

During this week, my client's take-home pay was $2250. Car 2 was traded for the client's sister's car which had no balance. This freed up $546 a month. To ensure there was no damage to the credit recovery process, the deal was that the sister would make the car payment to my client, who would then forward the payment to the lender.

This week, the two major credit cards were paid down by seventy percent. This transaction absorbed $1,355 of the take-home, leaving $895. The second installment account was eliminated, which took $490. This left my clients with $405. Of this money, $50 went to tithes and the rest to savings.

In addition, my clients performed some community service and worked in a ministry at their church to make up the difference of the tithes. The equivalent of $175 in tithes was spent in this effort.

The Fourth Week

Besides the mortgage and the remaining car, only $26,500 in debt remained—two medical bills, a student loan, and an installment loan. With the money freed from paying off the other debt, by now $1,000 extra a month could be applied to the debt reduction.

The take-home pay for this week was $1,250. Fortunately, my client was able to work the equivalent of $500 in overtime. So which remaining debt should they pay first? The student loan had a very low interest rate, but it was past due. The medical bills were in collection. The installment loan was current and, because it was an installment loan, it did not affect the credit score. I chose to work on the one that was most detrimental to the credit score: the student loan. If the late payments could be resolved, there stood an opportunity to have it totally removed from the credit report which would definitely boost the score.

On the credit report, it was showing that the balance of the loan was 121 payments in the amount of $106. Calculated, this amount was $12,826. Obviously, this was an error because the report showed that $7,522 was the balance. This gave us grounds for a dispute if we chose to go this route. Even though the loan was not reporting past due, we knew that it was past due because the date of last activity was showing as August 2006. At $106 per month, this loan was sixteen months past due and $1696 in arrears. It would take two weeks to bring it current.

This was the task for the next two pay periods. A payment in the amount of $850 would be made for the next two weeks. The goal was only to bring the loan current, not to pay it off. Once the loan was brought current, my client would pay $100.00 monthly for six months so that a positive payment history could be established with the Department of Education. Once established, a request would be made to have the negative history removed from the credit report, one of the benefits of the Department of Education's rehabilitation program (refer to Chapter Six). Afterwards, they are at the liberty to quick pay the balance using the techniques they had learned.

In lieu of tithing, the couple agreed to read to small kids at the library over the weekend and do the same at the daycare at church on Sunday. However, the weekly savings were met and $250 went into the savings account. The clients were left with $150 for the week.

The Fifth Week

This week my clients brought home $2250. The first thing we did this week was to clear the $850 past due on the student loan.

We were into a new month. Luckily the house sold. There was barely enough money to get rid of the house with closing and repairs coming from the proceeds. As the new house was not ready, we negotiated with the buyers to let my clients live in the house for thirty days rent–free as the house note would not be due for another thirty days after closing; and my clients signed a ninety-day lease at $1000 per month. Exempt from paying the mortgage this month, the normal mortgage payment went to pay the car note.

After paying the student loan and the car note, approximately $663 was left. Because it was the first of the month, these funds were used to pay utility bills and buy groceries, which amounted to nearly $550. For the first time, making payments to tithing and savings were exempt. My clients were left with $113 for the week.

The Sixth Week

Fortunately the husband was working overtime regularly now. He was motivated to pay down the debt. The teenage son had landed a job at the local fast-food joint. This alleviated the stress of trying to provide the extras that the teenager wanted while the parents attended to his necessities. This week, with overtime, the take-home pay was $1350.

The next thing to do was eliminate the $1500 medical bill. This debt had only been placed with a collection agency for two months at the time we started the cleanup. I was not hopeful that they were willing to settle so soon for pennies on the dollar.

Normally, when a settlement this drastic is achieved, it is because the contract with the collection agency has expired, and the medical facility just wants the debt removed from the books. This time, I would be dealing with the collection agency and not the medical facility. Nevertheless, I called with my usual twenty-five-cents-on-the-dollar offer. Just like I'd figured they would, they countered with ninety cents on the dollar. We settled on seventy-five. I accepted it. Why? Because they were asking $1350 initially and we only had to pay $1125. We remitted the $1125 to the collection agency which left my clients with $225.

The $9,000 debt was older. Because we waited a month before we tried to pay it off, the contract with the collection agency expired. Upon learning this, we immediately disputed the debt with the credit bureau. You see, because the collection agency no longer had jurisdiction over the debt, they could no longer report it to the credit bureau. Thus it would fall off of the credit report.

This does not mean that the debt was invalid; on the contrary, it was still due. We were just given a little time to pay it off. Remember one of the goals was to clean the credit in time to purchase the house. This debt would probably surface again because it was still relatively new—only two years old. Hopefully, it would not surface before we had time to settle with the medical facility to get it paid off. In the interim, we weren't going to worry about it.

From the $225 remaining, my clients donated $100 to the church. I thought it was only fair in light of the blessing of the $9,000-debt reprieve. No funds were deposited to the savings account this week.

When we began implementing the IPO strategy, we were on a sixteen-week deadline to pay down the debt and improve the credit score. As of the sixth week, all of the negative debt had been cleared and the only debt remaining was one car note and two small major credit cards, which we had reduced to thirty percent of the credit limit.

The debt was successfully reduced. One thing to note: even though the student loan was no longer in arrears, it would not be paid off for another six months. Why? I had my client postpone paying the loan off because by paying on time for six months, she would be in a position to have the negative history reporting from the student loan dismissed under the rehabilitation plan. Furthermore, she could use six months of positive history reporting in her file.

Now, we needed to acquire the credit report from a mortgage broker in order to get an accurate reading of the credit score. However, before we could do that, there was one more thing that had to be done: I disputed the debts as paid with the credit reporting agencies. The reason for this was that it normally takes the collection agencies sixty days to update the credit file. Had we let the mortgage company pull the credit report now, in the sixth week, there would not have been time to update the credit with the credit reporting agencies. This would have been a useless inquiry.

We did not want to wait the sixty days because we needed to get started on searching for a loan. By forcing the credit bureau to contact the creditors for an update, when the update was completed, a new credit score would be generated. At worst, the creditor would not get the information updated within the timeframe stipulated by the FCRA. If this occurred, the negative history would have to be deleted from the report entirely. We were in a win-win position.

As you can see from the synopsis of the debt-reduction process, not only did we eliminate the debt, but my clients always had money in their pockets. In addition, over the six-week period they had saved $939 and were able to contribute consistently to the church. This is the beauty of having a structured plan to manage cash flow.

Depiction of the Debt Reduction Strategy

Type of Debt	Week	Income	Orig. Debt.	Amt. Paid	Amt. Due	Savings Acct.	Tithe	Misc.
Medical	1	$2,250	$2,018	$539	0	$3,890	$225	$1,020
Visa	1		$1,890	$945	0			
Utility	2	$1,000	$807	$7,220	0	$1,000	$1,000	$78
Car Note 2	3	$22,500	$25,000	traded	0			
Visa	3		$1,400	$980	$420			
MasterCard	3		$536	$375	$161			
Install Acct. 2	3		$490	$490	0	$200	$100	$100
Student Loan	4	$1,250	$1,700	$850	$850	$250		$150
Student Loan	5	$2,250	$850	$850	0 (loan current)			
Car Note 1	5		$34,455	$687	$33,768			
Mortgage	5		$78,000	$78,000	0			
Misc. Bills	5		$550	$550	0	0	0	$113
Medical	6	$1,350	$1,500	$1,125	0	0	$100	$125
Medical	6		$9,000	0	0 (for now)			

The Seventh Week

The take-home pay in the seventh week was $2250. The husband did not work any overtime. He had earned the right to take a break. Their money issues had become a non-issue. My concern was that this couple would become too comfortable with the newfound freedom of being out of debt and fall back into their bad habits.

So this week we started working on the other goals in the Output column. To do this, a budget had to be established.

First, $225 was given to the church, and $410 went into savings. After these expenditures, my clients still had $1615 left over. There was $581 remaining on the major credit cards. Commencing with this week, all purchases charged on the major credit cards would be paid each month to avoid the interest on the cards. Thus out of this check, the $581 balance on the cards was paid in full. Subtracting this payment, a balance of $1034 was left.

Because my clients initially lacked discipline in spending their money, I advised them to open a separate account and entitle it "Household Account." This created a means to separate the money needed to run the household—mortgage, insurance, car note, groceries, etc.—from that which could be called "miscellaneous." With three accounts—savings, household, and miscellaneous—the money and its purpose would be uniquely separated. Thus the risk of spending money that should not have been spent was minimized.

The only funds that would remain in the household account were for paying bills. The funds in the miscellaneous account could be spent however the couple wished and the money in the savings account would be saved. To enforce discipline, I asked them to have the bank style the savings account as Mr. John Doe and Ms. Jane Doe, JTROS. In this manner, the funds in the savings account could not be accessed by either party without the other as long as both spouses are living. The JTROS — Joint with Rights of Survivorship — grants permission for the surviving spouse to access the funds when one of the spouses dies — then and only then. This may sound childish, but you would be surprised how just adding "and" to a joint account makes a difference when it comes to money matters in a relationship.

The Budget

A simple, semi-automated sample of a monthly budget which I created for you in a Microsoft Excel spreadsheet can be accessed from my website, www.theroadtocreditrepair.com. I have provided it as an example at the end of this section. It has two categories: Income and Expenses. Prefacing the Income category is a section for recording all of the wages earned for the month. The Income category exhibits money coming into the household or money earned: wages, interest, and business. The Expenses category exhibits money outgoing— for example, mortgage, insurance, utilities, car note, etc.

The best way to determine how money is going out is to balance your checkbook monthly. In this budget, there are three columns: 1) Budget Amount, the allowance for the month; 2) Actual Amount, the amount of money that was actually spent for the month; and 3) Difference, the difference between the amount budgeted and the actual amount. In other words, this column is calculated by subtracting column two from column one. For assistance with your budget, access my website, www.theroadtocreditrepair.com. There you have will access to many budgets and financial calculators.

This budget automatically calculates the amount of tithing and savings each month. Any additional income is automatically sent to the savings account. This budget was built around the client working overtime weekly. All income above the budgeted amount has ten percent extracted for tithing, prior to being sent to the savings account.

A negative number indicates that the actual amount spent was less than the amount budgeted. This is a very good thing. As the tithing and savings are automatically updated, this extra money can be spent for the enjoyment of the household. At the end of the month the savings account and tithing should be updated to include the computation in the budget.

Budget for John and Jane Doe

WAGES	Week 1	Week 2	Week 3	Week 4	Bonuses	
His	$1,350.00	$1,350.00	$1,350.00	$1,350.00	$500.00	$5,900.00
Hers	$1,000.00		$1,000.00			$2,000.00
TOTALS	**$2,350.00**	**$1,350.00**	**$2,350.00**	**$1,350.00**	**$500.00**	**$7,900.00**

Category / Income:	Budget	Actual	Difference
Wages	$ 7,000.00	$ 7,900.00	- $ 900.00
Interest	0.00	0.00	0.00
Small Business	0.00	0.00	0.00
Income Subtotal	$ 7,000.00	$ 7,900.00	- $ 900.00
Expenses:			
Mortgage	$ 2,300.00	$ 2,300.00	$ -
Insurance	$ 228.00	$ 228.00	$ -
Utilities	$ 400.00	$ 400.00	$ -
Car Note	$ 392.00	$ 392.00	$ -
Groceries	$ 240.00	$ 240.00	$ -
Gas	$ 400.00	$ 400.00	$ -
Daycare	$ 200.00	$ 200.00	$ -
Clothing	$ 200.00	$ 200.00	$ -
Lunch	$ 240.00	$ 240.00	$ -
Misc	$ 100.00	$ 100.00	$ -
Furniture	$ 200.00	$ 200.00	$ -
Expenses subtotal	$ 4,900.00	$ 4,900.00	$ -
Total Inc / Exp			$ (900.00)
Extra Money		$ 630.00	
Tithe		$ 790.00	
Savings		$ 1,580.00	

Summary

The couple in this example actually did not have money issues. They had an issue with being disciplined with their spending habits. However, once the desire to purchase a new home intensified, they realized, as I had in my situation, that they would never succeed as long as they were straddled with debt and a poor credit history. In this scenario, this was an easy fix because the money was plentiful and only direction and guidance in how to manage it was required.

Your situation may or may not be the same as this couple's. Perhaps your finances are worse—a lot worse. It does not matter. As long as you create an IPO strategy for your plan and then create a budget, you can eliminate your debt and improve your credit score.

If you are on a timeline, you may have to get a second job, work overtime, or start a small business. However, just know that the key to eliminating debt is two-fold: First, having a desire to get rid of the debt and second, having enough money to pay it off.

Once you determine how fast you want to pay off the debt, you must assure that there is enough income flowing to meet the deadline. In Chapter 10, I make suggestions for ways to increase your income so you can eliminate your debt sooner.

The Snowball Method

In Chapter 10, I cover debt reduction using another effective system: the snowball method, which involves a systematic meltdown of the debt from the smallest to the largest. The strategy I just presented involves assigning debt to a specific pay period and can be used when cash flow is not an issue and the debt needs to be paid rapidly.

Methods to Eliminate Your Debt by Yourself

Every exit is an entry somewhere.

— TOM STOPPARD

Close the door on the attitude of
I Can't Do It
to open the door to the one of
Yes, I Can!

— DEBORAH M. DENNIS

If you have built an IPO chart as described in Chapters 8 and 9, you can clearly see your goals (the OUTPUT). You can also see how much debt you need to pay off and how plausible it is for you to accomplish this with the resources you have, based on your current financial situation (the INPUT). You also laid out the steps you will take to eliminate the debt and ultimately improve your credit score (the PROCESS).

Don't be upset by your financial situation! As I've mentioned, you have taken the first big step toward eliminating all your debt by describing your financial situation, your plan, and your goals in writing in an IPO.

Now take a close look at your budget, which you prepared in Chapter 9, and see where you can cut expenses. If you did not prepare the budget, why don't you take a break and create one now? To get you started, you can visit my website at www.theroadtocreditrepair.com for access to a budget that can be saved for use with Microsoft Excel. To run the spreadsheet you will need at least Excel 97.

Do you really need to go out to dinner several nights a week or get take-out food? Can you lower your thermostat in the winter and raise it during the summer to spend less on heating and air conditioning? Can you shop at consignment stores for clothes for your kids? Go back to Chapter 7 and look at the list of wasteful spending, then apply it to your input numbers. Will that free up some cash at the end of each month?

Okay, maybe it won't free up enough to pay off your long-term debt in any reasonable length of time. So let's take a look at the other side of the equation: increasing your revenue. If you can't make more money at your current job and don't want to switch, here are just a few suggestions as to how you AND your spouse can add to your current income.

Twenty-two Ways to Find Extra Cash

1. Take in a roommate or boarder. Do you have an extra bedroom? A finished basement? Could the kids double up? A rent check at the end of each month from a person you know and can get along with can be a real help in paying your own rent or mortgage.

2. Take in a foster child. Your local human services agency is always looking for loving homes in which to place children on a temporary basis. The money isn't great but every little bit helps.

3. Use your talents for an at-home business. Could you give music lessons to kids? Art lessons? Tutoring? Teach English as a second language? How about a half-day play group for toddlers?

4. Provide a service. Even if you have a full-time job, there are services you can provide on nights and weekends. People are always looking for typists, editors and proofreaders, transcription services, tax preparation, medical billing assistance, graphic design, sitters for the elderly, house sitters, etc. Take some courses if you're not already an expert.

5. Sell stuff. In addition to holding a yard sale or selling jewelry or other family "heirlooms" that you really don't care about anymore, make buying and selling your business. Many people with an eye for value buy things cheap at yard or estate sales and then sell them on eBay for a profit.

6. Pet sitting. There is a huge need for people to walk dogs during the day or to take care of any kind of pet while owners are away on vacation. Get your kids to help.

7. Errands and other services. When both parents are working full-time, they end up having to run all their errands on the weekend or things just don't get done. Also many elderly people find it hard to get around. Offer to pick up dry cleaning, grocery shop, buy gifts, drive kids from school to practice, go to the post office, etc. Other people would love for someone to cook them meals that can be frozen and reheated for the following week. A simple ad in your local paper will get you started.

8. Speaking of the elderly, you can **be a companion or chauffeur.** It seems like so many of us live far away from our aging parents and would love for someone to do light housekeeping, cook, drive to medical appointments, pay bills or just stop by for a chat. Many would pay handsomely for this valuable service.

9. Outdoor services. Few people have the time or inclination to take care of their yards but they want them to look nice. Offer to weed or plant a garden, mow the lawn and fertilize, or to shovel snow in the winter. If you have a truck, invest in a snowplow attachment and you can plow driveways in the early morning, before you even go to work.

10. There are various **customer service or telephone sales jobs** that you can do from home if you have a computer and a landline. For some ideas, visit my website, www.theroadtocreditrepair.com, and click on Employment Opportunities.

11. Automobile detailing. If you like washing and working with cars you could do this at your customer's location. Find out what the local franchise detailers are charging and offer to do it for less.

12. Holiday decorations. Everyone wants their house to look great for the Christmas holidays but they don't want to get up on ladders and install lights, wreaths, etc. You could help customers come up with the design and then they will pay for all the materials.

13. Coaching. It's sad, but there are parents out there who don't have the time or inclination to teach their kids how to ride a bike, throw a fast pitch, or kick a football. A small ad in the local paper could get you some good business at the customer's home.

14. Courier. There is a huge need for companies, especially attorney's offices, to get documents and small packages from one place to another in a big hurry. Send email to office managers, upgrade your auto insurance if necessary, and pass out some business cards. You will get a lot of repeat business.

15. Sports trophies. I knew someone who did this out of his house and it was a great part-time business. Buy trophies wholesale and invest in a small engraving machine. Advertise to all the local Little Leagues as well as soccer and Pop Warner football teams.

16. Videography. Offer to take videos of weddings, kids' birthday parties, high school sporting events, etc. High school athletes also need someone to tape them so they can send DVDs to college recruiters.

17. Garage sales for others. Many people, especially elderly people who are getting ready to move to smaller quarters or a nursing home, do not have time to organize all the things they need to get rid of, price them, and run a garage sale. A small ad in the local paper or flyers could get you started.

18. Be a handyperson. If you are good at fixing things, painting, or doing small carpentry jobs, there are a lot of little things people need to have done around their houses and the larger repair companies don't want to be bothered doing small jobs.

19. Antique restoration. If you are good at fixing up old furniture and have a garage or barn to do the work in, antique dealers as well as homeowners will love to hire you.

20. Home monitoring. If you live near a seasonal resort area or a condominium development where half the people go someplace warm in the winter, offer to check up on their homes while they are away, and to take care of any problems. There is also a huge need for people to clean between rentals.

21. Participating in an MLM. There are several excellent multilevel marketing (MLM) jobs that will bring you extra money. For one, you can start a book club. I participate in an online book club that is an excellent way to increase income *and* simultaneously enhance literacy. In Chapter 17 I demonstrate the benefits of this venture that can involve the entire family.

22. Real estate sales. Because I'd been in the real estate business for so many years and had to find my own leads, perform my own marketing for the sale of my homes, become familiar with the laws governing real estate, and use my training as a mortgage-loan officer to find mortgage loans, I decided to get a real estate license.

It was easy obtaining the license. I called the state agency that regulated real estate agencies to ascertain the requirements for obtaining a license. After gathering the required information, I registered to complete the courses via correspondence. I took the classes via the computer and completed the coursework in five days.

In my state, if you have college hours, you may get an exemption from a couple of classes. I used my degree to qualify for this exemption and I only had to take five classes. I completed a class a day on the computer. Then when all of the courses were completed, I took the tests which were open-book. Once I passed the courses, I took the licensing pretest class. Then, I sat for the state exam. The entire process could very well take less than a month if you are serious about it.

I saved this for last because with a real estate license, you will have access to a tremendous database of homes for sale across a broad sales market. Once you get your credit straight, this type of license can prove invaluable if your goal is to acquire fixer-uppers to rent and/or as investments. Having a real estate license gives you an advantage over the investor who has to rely on an agent to do his "hunting."

Furthermore, with the high rate of foreclosures, an extremely lucrative business right now is handling short sales. My website, www.theroadtocreditrepair.com, is an excellent source to investigate real estate investing as a bona fide business for the entrepreneur at heart. Visit the site and click on Real Estate Investing Opportunities. There you will find information on how to get started using a coach.

So You Want to Become an Entrepreneur

When the world was introduced to ".com," we were given a very special gift. There is a wealth of information available for us to access over the Internet on the subject of home-based businesses and entrepreneurship.

If you are looking for a great place to just start exploring opportunities, check out my site, www.theroadtocreditrepair.com. From my site you can conduct research, find answers to questions, and explore opportunities by subject. You will find some great ideas for a home-based business as well as information on how to set up a business. At the home page, click on Starting a Business.

Couples Working Together Toward the End Goal

Chances are it took two of you to get into serious debt so it will take two of you to dig out of it. I think it's great when one parent is able to stay home with the kids and I wish I could have done it when my children were young. However, that doesn't let that spouse off the hook when it comes to increasing your income for debt elimination.

There are many home-based jobs that can be done even with babies and toddlers underfoot. In addition to some of the ideas I mentioned earlier, the first that comes to mind is childcare. You would not believe what people will pay for their child to be in a loving home with nice toys and other kids to play with.

The second is home-based selling with such companies as Avon, Tupperware, Mary Kay Cosmetics, Pampered Chef, Southern Living, Discovery Toys, Tahitian Noni, etc. Do you know why Tupperware was such a hit in the 1950's? Women were home with the kids, without their own cars, and they loved an excuse to get together. You can have these parties during the day or at night when your spouse is home. Let your imagination be your only roadblock when it comes to generating revenue.

If you are a stay-at-home mom with young kids, I invite you to visit my website, http://www.mybookwise.com/gemsoftomorrow/, to discover how you can start a bookstore business. If you are into health and wellness, Tahitian Noni is another great home-based venture for increasing revenue. In Chapter 17, I present in-home businesses as a viable means for increasing the household income.

Using Your Home Equity or Retirement Savings

It is very tempting to see a large pile of cash when you look at the current value of your home. If you subtract what you owe on your mortgage from what you think your home would sell for today, this is the amount of *equity* you have.

Banks are very comfortable giving out home-equity loans because if you don't repay, they can take your house. An additional benefit of a home-equity loan is that for most people, the interest you pay is tax-deductible, unlike the interest on a credit card or car loan. You can also make use of your home equity by refinancing at a lower interest rate and then taking cash out at closing.

I have let you in on my story enough for you to know that my husband and I tapped the equity in our home and manipulated other real estate investments to eliminate our debt. Short of hitting the lottery and inheriting a lot of money, I cannot think of a way to eliminate large amounts of debt quickly, within months, other than the use of equity from real estate. You only eliminate the debt if you sell the real estate; otherwise, you shift the debt. Sell or shift, it corrals the debt so that it can be managed if you do it correctly.

Some people will not agree with what we did but the facts are, the house had a lot of cash that could be tapped (equity) and we needed that cash to implement our dream and accomplish our goals. In the introduction to this book, you read how my husband and I were in debt over our ears, sold our house, and then built a new one with a lot of equity to use as a bank for future borrowing.

While this can be a great way to handle a temporary financial crisis or to avoid filing for bankruptcy, I do have some words of caution: *If you do not change your spending habits, you run the real risk of losing your house.* We have always understood this and this is the one area where we had tremendous discipline. It is one thing not to pay your credit cards on time and to have a low credit score, but it is quite another to become homeless. You worked hard to buy that house so the last thing you want to do is to go back to renting and start over to save money for a down payment. However, if you are ready to budget and control your spending, the equity in your home can be a lifesaver.

The other tempting pile of cash is what you have saved in a retirement plan. (You ARE saving for your retirement, aren't you? If you're not, don't worry! You will be, because part of my debt-reduction and reconstruction plan includes an automatic savings.) Yes, you can borrow from a plan such as a 401(k), but you need to pay it back. And if you happen to leave your job, you need to pay it all back before you go. Otherwise, you will be hit with very large tax penalties that will wipe out a good portion of what you have saved. Think carefully before you resort to this. Let this be your last option! However, it's preferable to filing bankruptcy. Just be sure to check with your CPA or another expert so that you know the full ramifications of your actions.

What to Pay Off—and What Not To

You may be in a position where whatever bill you are receiving the most heat about from debt collectors is the one you pay first. This is totally the wrong way to go about it. As you learned in the chapter that discussed bill collectors, Chapter Six, you can stop any harassment from them with a simple letter. Do not let them get you off track. Because you are paying off your debt, theirs will eventually get paid. Stick to your IPO!

There are other bills that will be ongoing while you are reducing your debt. These may or may not affect your credit score. You need to prioritize on an ongoing basis which bills need to be paid first in order to maintain your basic living requirements. In her book, *Your Credit Score*, Liz Pullman Weston advises that you divide all your bills into three main categories: essential, important, and non-essential.

Always pay your essential bills first:

Ten percent: Pay the church or share it with your favorite charity first, before you pay anyone else. An open fist allows blessings to flow in each direction. A closed fist doesn't let anything out; however, it doesn't let anything in, either. This is what I do. If you prefer not to give, continue to the next item and pay yourself. You can also give ten percent of your time to the church or to charity. The gift of giving does not have to be solely monetary. This may work for you if you need that extra ten percent for your debt reduction.

Twenty percent: Pay yourself twenty percent of your take-home pay. It doesn't matter if a bill collector calls. This may not be possible at first, but we sure are going to try hard to achieve this goal.

Now with the seventy percent that's left, this is how I want you to divvy the funds:

Mortgage or rent: You need a roof over your head. This goes for home-equity loans as well.

Insurance: Particularly car insurance. If you are uninsured and something happens, you are exposing yourself to all kinds of jeopardy. Insurance payments are at the top of the totem pole. You can lose your license or wipe out your assets if you're in an accident.

Child care: Also necessary if you require this in order to work.

Child support: You can go to jail if it's not paid.

Car payments and repairs: Essential if you need a vehicle to get to work.

Groceries: You have to eat but always take advantage of local food pantries and food stamps if you need them.

Utilities: You cannot live without electricity for lighting, cooling, heating, etc. By not paying these, you run the risk of having them shut off.

Important

Income taxes: You don't want to mess with the IRS, but you can work out payment plans.

Medical insurance: A medical crisis can also wipe out your assets.

Student loans: Lenders can garnish your wages if the loans are not paid.

Non-essential

Credit cards

Medical bills

Legal bills

Loans from friends and family: last but certainly not least.

The above items need to be paid if you have the money, but will not result in serious consequences, except to possibly affect your credit score, if you can't pay them on time. In particular, you can work out payment plans for medical and legal bills and they do not appear on your credit report unless you stop paying.

Many people are obsessed with paying down their mortgages as quickly as possible because they "hate being in debt." As I've mentioned, this is a good kind of debt because real estate will help in growing your money tree and the interest is tax-deductible as long as the mortgage is for your homestead or personal residence. Hopefully your home is growing in value each year because, if it is not, you're in trouble. Eliminate all of your other debts first and then concentrate on your mortgage. Interest on rental investments is also tax-deductible, as long as the property is leased.

Bargaining With Creditors

There are several ways that you can reduce the amount of debt you are paying by bargaining with creditors. Here are just a few:

1. Try to get a lower interest rate on your credit cards. This works better if you are doing business with a local bank that knows you well. If they refuse, look on the Internet or take advantage of any low-interest offers that come in the mail for other cards. Many are for zero-interest for a year or more. Then transfer your balance to the new card but don't cancel your old one. Keep in mind the consequences for maxing out a credit card. The goal is to keep the balances around the thirtieth percentile.

2. Bargain hard with your lenders for new payment plans. Before months have passed and bill collectors are calling, have frank conversations with high-level decision mak-

ers. Explain your circumstances and give the best sob story you can think of—whether it is unemployment or a medical crisis. Tell them it is only temporary, and that you would like to work out payment plans even if they are for a few dollars per week. Ask that your new arrangements not be noted as late payments on your credit report.

3. Refinance your mortgage loan. Always keep an eye on current interest rates which are constantly fluctuating. If yours is currently on the high side and you don't have prepayment penalties, there are many refinancing programs with no closing costs. If your current bank won't lower your mortgage interest rate, find a new one. Just bear in mind that refinancing is not free and it adds time to the number of years over which the mortgage is being repaid. Do the math, sometimes you could spend more money over the long run.

What If You Can't Pay It Off?

If you have tabulated, in your IPO, all of your current debts, projected your future earnings, figured out how to cut expenses and generate additional revenue, bargained with creditors to lower interest rates and monthly payments, and you still don't foresee paying off your debts within five years, you have several options:

Sell your house and buy a less expensive one. If you can do it on your own without hiring a real estate broker, you will save even more money. Some businesses will help you do this and only provide the services you need, such as inclusion on the Multiple Listing Service.

Take out a home-equity loan or borrow from your retirement plan, using the cautions mentioned previously. You can also set up a home-equity line of credit with your bank which will approve a specific amount of money that you can tap into and repay whenever you need it. Just make sure you make regular payments or you risk losing your house.

Temporarily reduce the amount you are paying into your retirement savings.

File for bankruptcy. Before you take this drastic step, consider using a credit-counseling service which we will talk about in the next chapter.

Get a second job or ask your employer for overtime. Then use this extra money to pay down the debt—not for living expenses unless you simply must.

Myth: Working With Lenders to Lower Rates Also Raises Your Credit Score

If you are already doing business with a lender and are just trying to get a lower interest rate, the most they will do is file a "soft" credit report request which will not affect your score.

The Method for Defeating the Madness: The Snowball Theory

There are many different methods that can be used to reduce debt. The conventional method of making payments each month until the debt is gone can be used, but with this method, you'll be old and gray by the time the debt is eventually paid. This is the long way.

In this section, I am going to introduce you to a common method

173

of paying off debt that doesn't take quite as long as the conventional method.

Imagine a small ball of snow rolling down a hill. As it descends it gets larger, continually rolling and rolling faster, incorporating each little particle in its path as it continues to the bottom of the hill, where it stops. When it stops, the small snowball is a big snowball, made up of snow and the debris that it picked up on its path along the way. As a matter of fact, it has become so large that you can throw it and take something out in the process. If the snowball is not kept on ice, it begins to melt, and in its liquid state, it is no more.

This theory can be likened to paying off debt. It is called the "snowball method of debt reduction"—a debt-elimination strategy made popular by Dave Ramsey, the national radio host. In his book, *The Total Money Makeover,* Mr. Ramsey advocates using the snowball method of debt elimination because, from a psychological point of view, success is more probable than using the traditional method.

The premise is that if debt is ordered from the least to the highest and the minimum payments are made on all of the debts in order, any extra money can be applied to pay the bill at the top of the list until it is paid in full. When this debt is paid in full, the money used in paying this debt can be coupled with the payment for the next debt on the list to pay it off, and so on and so on.

As the debts are eliminated, the money available to pay off the overall debt grows while the debt itself shrinks—just like the snowball grew as it rolled from one spot to the next down the hill and melted away with time. The more debt that is paid off, the more money there is for making payments and the faster the debt gets reduced.

This strategy of paying the minimum on accounts while simultaneously concentrating on the rapid payoff of a specific account is extremely effective in reducing debt using either of two theories: Starting with the debt that has the smallest balance and continuing toward the account with the largest balance, or reducing the debt with the largest interest rate first, then continuing to the account with the smallest interest.

The first method, the snowball method, is more psychologically gratifying because you can see more of the debt being paid off, which is encouraging. However, by using the second method, as you pay down the debt with the highest interest first, you are reducing the amount of dollars spent on interest, which saves money.

Let's look a little closer at the snowball strategy by analyzing the basic steps for its implementation. The process begins with paying the debt with the smallest balance first:

1. Organize all of your debt in order, from the smallest balance to the largest balance.

2. Create an IPO chart and list all of your income and all of your expenses in the INPUT column. Make note of all extra income. In the OUTPUT column, state your goal as the desire to be out of debt.

3. In the PROCESS column, write the strategy for paying off the debt (items 4 through 7 below).

4. Each month pay the minimum that is due on all accounts.

5. Send in the extra money with the payment for the account on the top of the list. You are going to add all of the extra income to the minimum payment for this account, and pay this amount on the bill until the debt is eliminated. Though the bill is paid, I don't want you to close the account. Your credit report needs to savor the benefit of having paid off this debt for a moment.

6. Remove this account from the list, and update the extra money for paying the bill at the top of the list by adding to this amount the payment that is available from the account that was just paid off.

7. If there are still names on the list, repeat the process from step 4; otherwise, *CONGRATULATIONS*—you are out of debt.

I chose to have you use this method because you need to be inspired to stick with it by physically watching accounts fall from the list faster—rather than having you save money by paying the debts with the highest interest rates first. If you are more concerned about saving money, then apply this principle by ordering your debt from the one with the highest interest rate to the one with the lowest interest rate. It is my personal opinion that you will realize a better chance for success if you use my preference. Either way, you have an organized method for quickly reducing your debt.

Using a Debt Calculator and Debt Reduction Spreadsheet

If you have a computer on which you can run Microsoft Excel 2000, you can access a free debt-reduction calculator through my website, www.theroadtocreditrepair.com. I use a debt-reduction calculator to automate the process of paying down the debt in the examples that follow. You will have no problem using this tool to model the reduction of your debt using the snowball method.

Let's look at an example that you can follow. First we construct an IPO.

IPO for Debt Reduction Using the Snowball Method

(Usual and customary bills are not considered here,
but should be included as part of the budget.)

Input	*Process*	*Output*
ASCERTAIN THE NET ASSETS INCOME	**THE PLAN: USE THE SNOWBALL METHOD FOR REDUCING THE DEBT**	**ENVISION THE GOALS:** To be debt-free.
Take-home pay: $3,500 his $2,500 hers Extra Money: $300	Each month, pay the minimum that is due on all accounts.	To build wealth through real estate. To create residual income.
DEBT GMAC $4,400 $250 Visa $15,000 $500 Mortgage $200,000 $1500 Ford $28,000 $888 Shell Visa $300 $24 Target $401 $35 MasterCard $14,000 $1250 Home Impr. $39,000 $1000	Send in the extra money with the payment for the account on the top of the list. Add all of the extra income to the minimum payment for this account, and pay this amount on the bill until the debt is eliminated. Remove this account from the list.	To become enlightened. To travel. To volunteer as a reader for the little ones at the elementary school.
POSITIVES Good Cash Flow Commitment to being successful Tired of living paycheck to paycheck	Update the extra money for paying the bill at the top of the list by adding to this amount the payment that is available from the account that was just paid off. If there are still names on the list, repeat the process from step 4. If there is no more debt, CONGRATULATIONS! You're free.	

Next, load the debt into the debt reduction calculator. The results should look like the sample below.

Balance Date:	9/1/2007			
CREDITOR INFORMATION TABLE				
Creditor	**Balance**	**Rate**	**Payment**	**Custom**
GMAC	4,400	13%	250	
Visa	15,000	13%	500	
Mortgage	200,000	7%	1,500	
Ford Motors	28,000	8%	888	
Shell Gas Visa	300	18%	24	
Target	401	18%	35	
MasterCard	14,000	9%	1,250	
Home Upgrade	39,000	18%	1,000	
Total:	**301,101**	Total:	**8,197**	
Monthly Payment:	**11,300**			
Initial Snowball:	$ 3,103			
Strategy:	1			

The calculator will automatically order the data to fit the snowball methodology; thus, you can enter the data freely, without the worry of sorting it first.

Enter the data at random. If you become confused, read the documentation on the right side of the spreadsheet. If, by chance, you accidentally erase one of the fields that are calculated automatically—

Total or Initial Snowball—just "undo" until the formula calculates a number; then proceed with your entries.

I offer this caution because if you inadvertently hit the space bar in one of these fields, it will erase the formula used to calculate the field. If this happens to you, don't panic. Just "undo" what you did, and start over.

As you enter the data, the spreadsheet updates; therefore, when you complete your entry, the second box will read as exhibited below:

Creditors in Pay-off Order	Original Balance	Total Interest Paid	Months to Pay Off	Month Paid Off
Shell Gas Visa	300	4.50	1	Oct-07
Target	401	6.02	1	Oct-07
GMAC	4,400	68.76	2	Nov-07
MasterCard	14,000	268.87	4	Jan-08
Visa	15,000	783.43	6	Mar-08
Ford Motors	28,000	1,347.99	10	Jul-08
Home Upgrade	39,000	4,517.31	12	Sep-08
Mortgage	200,000	24,032.83	30	Mar-10
Total Interest Paid:		**31,029.71**	(Lower is better)	

Because you provided the date that you started, the calculator tells you when your debt reduction process will end. It also tells you how long, in months, it will take to pay off the debt that bubbles to the top of the list as each debt is paid off. It considers all of the debt that you enter. If you enter your mortgage, the calculator will compute paying it off as well, using the money available.

According to this scenario, this individual was out of debt in less than three years, inclusive of mortgage. In the process, $31,029.71 in interest was paid. In this example, the individual had a lot of money to contribute toward the debt reduction. Let's look at the same situation, but with an amount of money available per month that is significantly less, and more realistic.

Balance Date:	9/1/2007			
CREDITOR INFORMATION TABLE				
Creditor	**Balance**	**Rate**	**Payment**	**Custom**
GMAC	4,400	13%	250	
Visa	15,000	13%	500	
Mortgage	200,000	7%	1,500	
Ford Motors	28,000	8%	888	
Shell Gas Visa	300	18%	24	
Target	401	18%	35	
MasterCard	14,000	9%	1,250	
Home Upgrade	39,000	18%	1,000	
Total:	**301,101**	Total:	**4,322**	
Monthly Payment:	**4,622**			
Initial Snowball:	$ **300**			
Strategy:	**1**			

This example represents a two-income family with middle-class status that had an additional $300 left at the end of the month, which could be applied to their bills. The calculator processed the input and output the following results:

Creditors in Pay-off Order	Original Balance	Total Interest Paid	Months to Pay Off	Month Paid Off
Shell Gas Visa	300	4.50	1	Oct-07
Target	401	11.31	2	Nov-07
GMAC	4,400	264.81	9	Jun-08
MasterCard	14,000	2,056.74	30	Mar-10
Visa	15,000	3,154.12	33	Jun-10
Ford Motors	28,000	3,519.60	34	Jul-10
Home Upgrade	39,000	16,926.84	41	Feb-11
Mortgage	200,000	71,997.42	87	Dec-14
Total Interest Paid:		97,935.34	(Lower is better)	

The calculator outputs the amount of interest paid. However, the real effect of paying off the mortgage early cannot be seen from this example. An amortization calculator provides this information. These and other financial calculators can be accessed from my site.

However, notice that this couple became completely debt-free in a little over seven years, inclusive of the mortgage payoff. By paying off the mortgage early, they saved approx. $257,000 in interest (assuming that the mortgage was taken out just prior to the date of the beginning of the debt reduction).

Using the amortization calculator to generate an amortization schedule, it was shown that the interest over 360 months, on a principal loan of $200,000 at 8.23 percent interest, would have been

$339,899.95. The example below illustrates the powerful effects of having paid the mortgage in full, twenty-three years ahead of time:

Monthly Payment:	**$1500.00**
Total interest over the life of the mortgage:	**$339,899.95**
Average interest each month:	**$944.17**
Approximate interest paid after eighty-seven months:	**$82,142.79**
Overall savings in interest:	**$257,757.16**

Cha-ching!

Exercise Diligence in Using the Snowball Method

The snowball method is perfect for eliminating debt quickly when the will is there and you are just fed up with not enjoying the money you make because you have to pay those awful bills.

There are two caveats to be aware of. The first is that the snowball method will only work if you don't continue adding to your current debt. Cut up your credit cards, saving one for emergencies, or put them in a place you can't easily get to. However, do not close the accounts; use this good payment history to improve your credit score.

During the process of resolving the debt, make a commitment not to spend the money reserved for use in the snowballing process, unless you make or earn extra. Don't depend on future inheritances, tax refunds, bonuses, lottery winnings, etc., to bail you out. If you are blessed to receive extra money from these sources, put it in your savings account, or use it to further pay down your debt.

The other caveat is that the snowball method is for debt elimination. If your main goal is to increase your credit score, you may be better off paying down each debt to thirty-five percent of the credit limit first. Once you reach that point for each debt, start with the next debt on your sorted list. Remember, during this process: do not add any debt to your list and, above all, be guided by the Ten Commandments that follow:

Ten Commandments for Healthy Credit

Thou shall become a positive and possibility thinker, shall develop a love for money like thou love thyself, and shall learn to appreciate the value of its importance.

Thou shall, from this day forth, work diligently to reduce thy debt, improve thy credit score, and build wealth through multiple streams of income.

Thou shall develop an IPO strategy and use the tools presented in this book to reduce thy debt and maintain healthy credit.

Thou shall save all excess funds and stop wasting money.

Thou shall have only one major credit card, one installment account, and at least one real estate loan in good standing on thy credit report at all times. Thou shall not quit trying to become a homeowner.

Thou shall limit the use of revolving credit and shall never charge more than 35% of the credit limit, ever.

Thou shall pay all of thy bills on time. Period.

Thou shall block all inquiries from thy credit report by not letting anyone pull thy credit, unless it is an emergency.

Thou shall never cosign a loan for anyone.

Thou shall monitor thy credit report at least annually
and each time thou feel something is wrong.

In Chapter 11 we will explore in detail the option of working with
a credit counseling agency.

CHAPTER 11

Working With a Credit Counseling Agency

*The man who gets the most satisfactory results
is not always the man with the most brilliant single mind...*

— W. ALTON JONES

When I was experiencing my financial crisis, I was fortunate to have friends in the right places who could give me advice. These included bankers, real-estate professionals, mortgage brokers and financial planners. However, not everyone has this luxury. If you feel as though everything is spinning out of control, and you need help because you've tried my IPO and the snowball method without any results or relief, there are genuine credit counseling agencies that can be of great assistance. There are also a lot of dishonest credit repair agencies out there, so you need to be very careful about whom you select.

Credit counseling agencies can do anything from preparing a monthly budget for you and paying your bills to negotiating with your creditors on your behalf. They do charge a fee for their services, so unless you feel totally incapable of managing your own finances, there are many things you can do on your own—especially after reading this book!

Are You a Candidate?

First, let's try to determine if you really do need outside help. Take this little quiz and you will be better able to decide if you can go it alone with a little self-discipline, or if it would be easier if someone else took control of your finances for a while.

Do you pay your bills only when threatened with utility shut-offs or hounded by bill collectors?

Do you lose sleep at night worrying about all the debt you are carrying?

Have you resorted to gambling (including large purchases of lottery tickets) as a way to solve your financial situation?

Are you constantly being hit with late charges because you are careless about paying your bills on time?

Do you cringe whenever the phone rings, knowing it is probably a bill collector calling?

Are you frequently fighting with your spouse over money issues?

Is your mailbox filled with past due notices?

Are you unable to make even the minimum monthly payments on your credit card bills?

Do you borrow from one card to pay off another?

Are you constantly dipping into your reserve credit on your checking account with no hope that you'll be able to pay it back?

If you answered "yes" to one or more of these questions, you are probably a candidate for credit counseling services. Here are some of the services a counseling agency can provide:

Negotiating with your lenders to get lower interest rates, waived late fees or smaller minimum payments each month.

Paying all your bills on your behalf. You will pay them a specific amount each month to cover your bills, plus a small service fee.

Working with you to design a budget you can live with.

Developing a long-term savings plan.

Teaching you how to avoid financial problems in the future.

Now, the trick is to find a counseling agency that is going to provide an honest service and not try to rip you off and put you further into debt.

Counseling Services Versus Repair Agencies/Doctors

The first thing to look for when selecting an agency is whether they call themselves a "credit counseling" service, or "credit repair" or a "credit doctor." You want a credit counseling service. Credit repair agencies will offer to get copies of your credit reports and consolidate them for a fee which, as we know, is very easy to do yourself. They may also claim that they can remove bad debts from your reports but, sometimes, when an investigation is going on about a credit report dispute, a debt disappears temporarily, so don't fall for that trick. They may also claim they can reduce your credit card debt by anywhere from ten to fifty percent.

Don't fall for any ads, especially on the Internet, that offer to instantly wipe out all your debts and remove any negative information from your credit reports. Here are some other red flags to look for:

Requiring large monthly service charges.

Telling you not to contact your creditors or to stop making payments before your debt management plan is set up.

Claiming that your creditors will never sue you for unpaid debts.

A recent IRS audit of credit repair companies found that forty percent were not eligible for the non-profit status they were claiming which is possibly an indication that unscrupulous activities were going on. Under the Credit Repair Organization Act, a company cannot require you to pay in advance for any services until they have been completed. You must be given a written contract clearly describing all your rights and obligations; also, a copy of the pamphlet "Consumer Credit File Rights Under State and Federal Law" must be given to you before you sign any contract.

The Good and the Bad

In order to separate the good from the bad, look for an agency that is accredited by the Consumer Credit Counseling Services (CCCS), the National Foundation for Credit Counseling, or the

Association of Independent Consumer Credit Counseling Agencies. The agency's employees should be completely trained in all aspects of consumer credit and money and debt management. Many states now require them to be licensed. Take the extra step to check with the Better Business Bureau (http://www.bbb.org), or your state's attorney general's office, to make sure that no complaints have been filed against the agency you're looking at.

Once you select one, it is important to give them a complete picture of all your debts, income, and expenses so they can help prepare a realistic budget and payment plans to meet your particular needs.

Your Score May Be Worse Before It Gets Better

It is true that some lenders will indicate that they are being paid by a credit counseling service and that a notation will be made on your credit report. Other potential lenders will see this as a good thing as there is probably a better chance they will be paid in the future.

If your credit counseling service plan is designed so that you are making less than full payments as agreed to by the lender, these may still temporarily show up as late on your report. Once you are caught up, this notation will be removed. At this point, sitting back and not doing anything to improve your financial situation is far worse than a notation on your credit report stating that you are working with a credit counseling agency.

Costs

As we have seen, many credit counseling firms advertise themselves as non-profit, but that doesn't mean that their services are free or inexpensive. Unsavory credit repair agencies are out there and they may try to charge high, hidden fees or encourage you to make voluntary contributions. If any of these red flags appear with an agency you are considering, run for the nearest exit.

Your best bet is to find a credit counseling agency that will let you meet with a counselor in person. You can find legitimate ones through a local university, a military base, a housing authority, your bank, a branch of the U.S Cooperative Extension Service, a credit union, or a local consumer protection agency. One of the requirements of filing for bankruptcy is to meet with a credit counseling service and the U.S. Trustees Program keeps a list of approved agencies.

Once you have interviewed and chosen a firm to work with, a credit counselor will review your complete financial situation and help you develop a personalized plan that is tailored to your specific needs. One of your service options in credit counseling—called a debt management plan— allows you to make one lump-sum payment each month and then have the service pay all your bills for you. If you take advantage of this service, make sure you continue to check with your creditors each month to verify that payments are being made on time.

For this service the agency will charge a small monthly fee and, to set up a monthly plan, the cost should be around $50. Avoid agencies that ask for large, upfront payments for any services. And if you really can't afford to pay anything and the agency says that they can't help you, look for another agency.

A good debt management plan could take four years or even longer to clear up past debts, based on your current income and expenses. In the meantime, you have to agree not to continue adding or using any new types of credit while working with the credit counselor.

Nine Key Questions to Ask

Before agreeing to work with a credit counseling agency, be sure to ask these nine questions:

What services do they offer and how much will each service cost? Get all the details in writing before you agree to use their services. You want to know what each item costs and if there are any upfront charges. If they say that credit counseling, or paying less than you owe, will not have a negative effect on your credit report, this is a red flag and the agency should be avoided.

Will you be signing a formal contract detailing all the services to be provided, including associated costs? If they don't offer you a detailed, written contract, keep looking for another agency. Ask if there are any upfront set-up fees and monthly service charges and if they will be paying bills on your behalf. Make sure all verbal promises are put in writing.

Is the credit counseling agency licensed in your state and have any complaints been filed with the attorney general's office or the Better Business Bureau? Doing your homework now can save a lot of trouble later by helping you to avoid disreputable agencies.

Are the individual credit counselors licensed in your state? Many states require this for anyone offering credit counseling or other debt management services. Counselors should have received training and certification from an outside organization.

How are the credit counselors paid? If they are on commission, they will be more inclined to sell you all kinds of services you may not need.

In addition to paying your monthly bills, will the agency offer ongoing budgeting advice? You want not only to correct the mistakes of the past, but learn how to avoid them in the future.

How often will you receive status reports on bills paid on your behalf? Ideally, you can get up-to-date, detailed information online or by phone.

Are there any debts they won't be paying on your behalf? There may be some types of debt the agency cannot pay, so you will have to continue paying these on your own.

Are all the deposits you send them fully insured against loss or misappropriation? You want the money you send to a credit counseling agency to be protected.

Weigh Your Options

Now you know that credit counseling can be a valid option for digging out of a financial hole. Go back to the questionnaire at the beginning of this chapter and ask yourself again if you think you need outside help or if you can handle it alone.

If you think you can pay off your debts within five years and you generally pay your bills on time, with a little self-discipline, you are probably a good candidate for managing your own finances. However, if you consistently pay your bills late, if you have bill collectors calling, if your credit score has plummeted, or if your spending is out of control, there is no shame in asking for help. Your main goal may be to avoid filing bankruptcy which we will be talking about in the next chapter.

- CHAPTER 12 -

Filing for Bankruptcy

*When the day is dark
and the sun stops shining,
God puts a rainbow in the cloud.*

—FATHER TIMOTHY GOLLOB

When my husband and I hit bottom in managing our finances, after our first housing development was in jeopardy of failing, we did briefly consider filing for bankruptcy. We eventually decided against it because more than our well-being was at stake and a bankruptcy would remain on our credit report for ten years. We had worked too hard becoming creditworthy. Besides, our creditors had given us a second chance and we felt obligated to ensure that they were paid.

You may be in a different situation and bankruptcy is certainly an alternative you should consider. As I mentioned in the previous chapter, credit counseling agencies can offer such services as reviewing your debts versus expected income so they would be in a good position to advise you whether or not you should start talking to an attorney who specializes in bankruptcies.

We hear a lot about filing for bankruptcy in the news, but what exactly is it? Bankruptcy is a legal process in which an individual or business in financial trouble can work out a plan to pay their debts under the protection of a bankruptcy court. A court may decide that you are unable to pay all your debts and can officially cancel or "discharge" them.

In addition to the questions you answered in the previous chapter on credit counseling, you can ask yourself the following to see if bankruptcy is something you might need to pursue:

Is your house about to be foreclosed on or are you facing eviction from your apartment for nonpayment of rent?

Is the car you need to get to work about to be repossessed?

Has your salary been garnished to pay a debt?

Are you facing a lawsuit for not paying a debt?

Do you have a large amount of medical bills that you know you'll never be able to pay off?

Have you been out of work for a long time, with bills piling up?

Are your utilities about to be shut off?

Do you have a large amount of student loan debt that you know you'll never be able to pay, based on salaries earned in your profession?

Are there creditors trying to collect more money than you really owe?

Are you constantly being harassed by bill collectors?

If you answered "yes" to one or more of these questions, you may want to seriously consider speaking with a bankruptcy attorney.

What Kinds of Bankruptcy Are There?

There are two types of bankruptcy that you can file for: Chapter 7 and Chapter 13. You may have also heard of Chapter 11 but this is something businesses utilize to give them time to reorganize and to pay their creditors.

Chapter 7 involves selling your nonexempt assets (more about this in a minute) and using the proceeds to pay your debts. Most people filing Chapter 7 do not have a lot of non-exempt assets so they can get a fresh start with many debts discharged relatively quickly—several months after filing. Most of their debt will be from credit cards, medical bills or certain types of student loans. These are known as "dischargeable" debts. If you do own a home or a car, you can sign an agreement that you will continue to make payments on these, so you get to keep them.

Chapter 13 is for people with regular incomes who need more time to pay their bills, which are usually secured debts such as mortgage payments or car loans. Secured debts are those that have tangible property attached to them. Chapter 13 filers also have substantial assets such as jewelry, artwork, or family heirlooms that they don't want to be forced to sell under Chapter 7; or, they have debts that are not "dischargeable," such as taxes. The main goal for a Chapter 13 filer is to get better terms, such as lower or no interest on the debts they have already incurred. The person filing has five years to pay back the debts under the supervision of a bankruptcy court.

What State You Are Living in Matters

Federal laws state that there are certain items that cannot be taken, in a bankruptcy case, in order to pay off the filer's debts.

However, it is up to each state to decide what is exempt (cannot be taken and sold) and what is nonexempt. For example, in New York state, the following are exempt:

Any property owned and used as a primary residence.

Clothing, household items such as furniture, stove, television or refrigerator, pets worth up to $450, wedding rings.

Cash up to $2500.

Pensions and other retirement plans.

Security deposits for rent and utilities.

Ninety percent of wages earned within sixty days of filing a bankruptcy petition.

The right to receive benefits such as unemployment compensation, disability payments, Social Security, public assistance, and crime victim's awards.

How Does Bankruptcy work?

Filing for bankruptcy is something you can do on your own, but I would advise against it. The procedure can be rather complicated and time consuming and you want to make informed decisions every step of the way. First, do your own research at your local library or bookstore to educate yourself and then speak with an attorney who specializes in this area. He or she can suggest the best course of action for your situation.

If you decide to go forward with filing for bankruptcy, you first need to decide which kind is most appropriate for you—Chapter 7 or Chapter 13. If you believe you would be able to pay your past debts if you had more time and reduced interest charges, then Chapter 13 is probably the way to go. If you will be unemployed for the foreseeable future or are disabled, Chapter 7 may be the best choice.

The next task will be to pull all your information together in order to file a voluntary petition. This includes all your debts, assets, possible sources of income, and monthly expenses. It is very important to list all your debts and assets since, if you leave out an asset, it could be sold; if it is a debt, you could end up paying it on your own.

Numerous forms will be filled out by your attorney and then the petition will be filed with the court. A trustee will be appointed by the court, this person will oversee all payments to your creditors, and decide who gets how much money and when. He or she will ensure that all necessary information is collected from you and that everything is accurate.

You and the court will then notify all your creditors that you have filed for bankruptcy. At this point, all actions against you such as car repossession, foreclosure, wage garnishments, lawsuits, and contact from bill collection agencies, must stop. Later on in the process, you may be meeting with your creditors or their attorneys, along with the trustee and your attorney to work out payment solutions.

If you are filing Chapter 13, you must start paying the trustee handling your case within thirty days of filing your payment plan. A budget will be approved that shows what you can afford to pay over sixty months. Some unsecured creditors may not receive the full amount they are owed. The trustee will then pay your approved creditors on a regular basis for the sixty-month period.

With Chapter 7, the court will decide which creditors will be paid based on the proceeds from the sale of your non-exempt assets. A creditor can challenge any discharged debt and can claim that you committed a theft or fraud in your dealings with them. Once the court determines the final payments, it will mail to both you and your creditors the notice of which debts were discharged. Always keep a copy of this document as you may need it in the future to prove to your creditors that you are no longer responsible for the debt.

What Does Bankruptcy Eliminate?
(And What Does It Not?)

Filing for bankruptcy will eliminate or pay off many types of debt such as credit cards, medical bills, and unsecured loans. However, you are still responsible for paying other debts such as child support, alimony, and taxes. Here is a list of debts that are non-dischargeable in most states:

Taxes and tax penalties for the past three years.

Debts for luxury items purchased within sixty days of filing your bankruptcy petition.

Alimony and child support.

Fines and penalties of a government agency.

A debt you forgot to list on your petition.

Restitution you are required to pay as a result of committing a crime.

Student loans guaranteed by a government agency or a non-profit institution.

Debts for personal injury or death caused by your drunk driving.

Who Qualifies?

It is up to the bankruptcy court to decide if you qualify based on your projected income and expenses. There are now income limits on who can file for Chapter 7 but it will be easier to file for Chapter 13.

Basically, if you feel you can't pay off all your unsecured debts within five years and you don't have much equity in your home, bankruptcy is something you may want to pursue. However, it may not make sense if any of the following apply to your financial situation:

Most of your debts can't be discharged (canceled) such as government-guaranteed student loans, child support, and recent taxes.

You defrauded your creditors by lying on a credit application about your income or other debts.

You recently purchased luxury items or took an expensive vacation when you clearly could not afford it.

You want to file for Chapter 7 but filed for bankruptcy within the past six years. However, you can file for Chapter 13 at any time.

How Much Does It Cost?

Filing for bankruptcy will cost about $300 in addition to $1,000 to $2,000 for attorney's fees. You should be able to receive a free initial consultation from your attorney.

The more complete and accurate you can make your list of assets, expenses, income, and debts, the more money you will save. In some states it is not necessary for the attorney to attend all the meetings with your creditors, so if you feel comfortable enough, this is another area wherein you can save money.

Requirements Under the New Bankruptcy Laws

You've probably heard about the new bankruptcy legislation that took effect on October 17, 2005 and the rush of people trying to file before that date. Some experts believe that the law will benefit you, the debtor, while in other aspects, it limits the number of people who can file Chapter 7.

Now, only people who fall under the median state income, adjusted for family size as well as inflation, and those who pass a vigorous means test will be eligible to file for Chapter 7 bankruptcy. Otherwise, you will be required to file for Chapter 13 with a mandatory five-year term for court supervision before any debts can be discharged.

Also required under the new law is that anyone considering filing for bankruptcy must receive counseling from an approved credit counseling agency to evaluate all other options. The new laws were put in place to encourage people to pay their creditors rather than take what they may see as an easier way out by filing for bankruptcy.

Is It Worth It?

In my opinion, bankruptcy should be the solution of last resort. It can do serious damage to your credit history, making it difficult to obtain credit in the near and distant future. It will be much more difficult to buy a house or to obtain a car loan. Also, as we have seen, both future employers and insurance companies are looking at credit reports as part of their decision making process.

You will not be able to get a discharge on your new debts for another six years, so you need to think about what would happen if you had a sudden job loss or medical crisis during that time. Take a good look at your current financial picture, see a reliable credit counselor, and then decide if the short-term advantages outweigh the long-term disadvantages.

Alternatives to Bankruptcy

One of the main reasons people file for bankruptcy is that they are about to lose their homes to foreclosure. They came into the situation due to overspending, a medical crisis, divorce, or a job loss. However, before you take the drastic step of filing for bankruptcy protection that will affect your ability to get credit in the future, consider other ways to protect your home.

The first question to ask yourself is whether this is a temporary financial crisis or if the mortgage is something that you will never be able to afford. Perhaps you could negotiate more time or better payment terms with your lender, to get you through a temporary crisis.

Here are some other ways you could ward off foreclosure before you resort to filing for bankruptcy:

Refinance. Perhaps you took out an adjustable loan or a balloon mortgage and now your payments have increased beyond your ability to pay. If interest rates are favorable and you have enough equity in your house, consider refinancing for a lower interest rate.

Negotiate with your lender. You may be surprised to find out that your bank or mortgage company is willing to renegotiate the terms of your loan, particularly if they know it is a temporary situation due to a job loss or medical crisis. Call and ask to speak with a senior decision maker, and tell them you are considering filing for bankruptcy if there are no other alternatives. Foreclosures and bankruptcies will cost them a lot more money than will working with you to come up with a new payment plan. You could also ask for a temporary suspension of your payments or a reduced monthly amount until you are back on your feet again. Make sure all verbal agreements are put in writing.

Borrow from family and friends. As long as you can commit to paying the money back, there is no shame in asking family or friends for a temporary loan. Write up a formal contract with a specific timeline of dates and amounts that you will be paying. Someday, you will be able to return the favor.

Sell your house. This is what my husband and I decided to do, since we had a lot of equity and it freed up some cash. We had a dream and we didn't mind moving to a smaller house. We later built a house that we used as collateral for future loans. Any real estate agent would be happy to come over and give you an estimate on what your house would sell for in today's market. You might be pleasantly surprised!

Myth: Bankruptcy builds a wall between you and all future credit.

Fact: It will be possible to get credit even after you file for bankruptcy. Secured credit cards can be obtained, for which you put a certain amount of money into a savings account as collateral. Once the bankruptcy has been discharged, you will have a fairly decent credit score if you pay your bills on time. Slowly rebuild your credit and you will be in a good position to purchase a home. The ability to purchase a home will be more probable if the loan-to-value (LTV) is in favor of the lender.

Re-establishing Your Credit

Once your bankruptcy process is complete, you will have the opportunity to make a fresh start. Your goal will be to manage your finances better so you don't end up in the same situation in the future. Getting credit for the next ten years will be more difficult with a bankruptcy notation on your credit report, but certainly not impossible. Take the following steps and you will be well on your way toward a bright credit future.

Pay all your bills on time. If you can do this for at least eighteen months, it will go a long way toward increasing your credit score.

Get a job. Even if it's a part-time position, you want to demonstrate that you can hold down a job and have a steady income stream.

Get copies of your credit reports and submit an explanation. As we have seen in previous chapters, it is important to constantly monitor your credit report, to ensure no errors are on it. If you find incorrect information, have it fixed immediately. Also, you can submit a statement of about 100 words, explaining why you had to resort to filing for bankruptcy. This might have been due to a serious illness or accident, or the loss of a job.

Open a savings account and a checking account. Future creditors love to see people putting regular deposits into a savings account or money market, even if it's only a few dollars a week. You also want to demonstrate that you can manage a checking account by not bouncing checks.

Get rid of unnecessary credit cards. It is much too tempting to overspend if you have a lot of credit cards lying around with zero balances. Keep one gas card, one department store card, and one for general use, such as

Visa or MasterCard. If you don't have any open credit accounts, apply for a secured credit card if you are having difficulty getting credit approvals.

Many people wonder if they will ever be able to qualify for a mortgage after filing for bankruptcy. If you have a steady income, pay your bills on time and limit the amount of debt you are carrying, the answer is definitely "yes." It may take you longer and you may end up paying a higher interest rate, but if you follow the steps listed above, you can certainly qualify.

Experts believe that two years after you file for bankruptcy, you are eligible for mortgage loans with terms as good as those given to people who have not filed. The size of your down payment and a steady income will be much more important than the fact that you once filed for bankruptcy.

You should also keep in mind that your spouse is not affected by your filing for bankruptcy if he or she did not cosign an agreement or contract for any of your debts—in most states. However, if you had put in a request for an additional credit card in his or her name, as a joint owner, then he or she would be responsible for the debt.

On the other hand, the following community property states do not require both parties to have signed a contract in order to be held responsible, unless it is for the purchase of real estate. Then, both spouses must have signed. Here are the states: Arizona, California, Idaho, Nevada, New Mexico, Texas, Washington, and Wisconsin. So, be careful if you marry an uncontrolled spender in any of these states!

Myth: Bankruptcy fixes your credit.

Fact: Bankruptcy is a major step to take and it will stay on your credit history for ten years. It's an opportunity to get a fresh start but will not erase problems from the past.

Speaking of the past, let's take a look at how you can avoid over-spending and living beyond your means by going "back to the basics with budgeting." Even if you only do the exercise once a year, it's a great way to plan for ongoing as well as surprise expenses and to save for your future.

- CHAPTER 13 -

Mastering Your Budget

Good habits result from resisting temptation.

—Ancient Chinese Proverb

Throughout this book, and in particular when we talked about using my IPO strategy, I have mentioned the importance of making a monthly budget and sticking to it the best you can. This helps prevent running short each month and enables you to target money to put aside for future savings and cash emergencies. I realize it is a pain to do, but once everything is set up, it shouldn't take more than a few hours each month to manage.

There are many great reasons to create a budget; here are just a few:

Before a building is built or a new road created, there is a plan. This ensures that everyone will not be running off in different directions and getting distracted from the main task. The same goes for debt reduction which is why I developed the IPO strategy. And the same goes for a budget. If you can set up a plan for how you intend to spend your money each month, you can maintain your focus on your end goal of saving or of paying off debts. Seeing how your money is spent will help with the manner in which you spend it.

A budget that is contributed to by the whole family prevents a lot of arguments over how money is spent. If a certain amount is budgeted for food, clothing, dining out, and children's entertainment, whoever wants to make a change and/or overspends has to subtract it from something else—particularly something that adversely affects what that person needs or wants.

It will be far easier to track where all the money goes. If you feel you are living paycheck to paycheck and never have anything left over, you will be able to see why right before your eyes.

It helps you reach your long-term savings goals because you can set up a certain amount to save and then work backwards from there to see where you need to trim in order to put aside this amount.

A budget will help ensure that you are setting up an emergency fund. The people who get themselves into financial trouble usually have not saved for a rainy day.

A good budget will enable you to see where you are wasting money. The challenge is to update it regularly.

Setting Up a Budget You Can Live With

In order to set up a realistic budget, you need to precisely predict and record what your monthly expenses will be. Start your budgeting project by gathering together pay stubs, your checkbook going back one year, and old bills, if you need them. From my website you can access a spreadsheet that can be used to keep track of your budget. This spreadsheet can be saved on your hard drive and it can be edited and updated using Microsoft Excel. It is completely automated and it updates certain fields automatically. Note: you will need Microsoft Excel, no older than version 97–2003, to run the software.

As you saw from the example in Chapter 9, this worksheet automatically calculates tithing, savings, and the difference between the budgeted amount and the actual amount spent. This is a simple budget that lumps all expenses not defined into a single category called "Misc."

In this chapter I offer a more detailed budget. This is the version provided on my website. Remember, you can edit the budget by adding or deleting the rows as necessary. Either way, simple or more detailed, with a budget, you will know exactly where your money is going without having to estimate, which is a lot less accurate.

First, get an exact account of what your take-home pay is. To this add any extra income you expect to receive in the next twelve months, based upon past history. This might include a bonus, interest income from a bank, dividends from stocks that are not reinvested, or money from a small business that you started. At the beginning of the spreadsheet is an area to record this information. It is known as the Input Section.

Remember from the IPO strategy, that you cannot fix or work on something unless you know what you have to work with. What you have to work with, your income, is the Input that you need to do the Process of creating and carrying out the budget. The Output is successfully living according to the budget monthly—the goal.

Next, enter your fixed expenses. These will be easy to find by looking in your checkbook. (Even if you pay your bills online, you should be writing them down in your checkbook.) This is also considered input because, again, you must always know what you are working with. Fixed expenses include such items as rent or mortgage, home, car, and other insurance, property taxes, Internet services, cable TV, tuition, etc. Some fixed costs are only due quarterly or once or twice a year. Since you don't want to have to come up with the full amount in the particular month that it is due, divide each amount by twelve. Then, account for it in the budget.

Variable costs will be a little harder to pin down. These include phone, food, clothing, pet care, entertainment, etc. This is where past spending records from your checkbook and credit card bills will come in handy. Be as accurate and honest as you can when projecting what these amounts will be.

Last, put in an amount for your savings goals, whether they are for a house, retirement, or college. Experts always recommend paying yourself first. If you have payroll deductions that go directly into a retirement plan or other savings accounts, you will not see it and will not be tempted to spend it on other things. If you are already doing this, add a line item for general savings and of course, for your emergency stash of cash, which we will be talking about in a minute. The spreadsheet will guess at this amount monthly, based on what is left after your bills are paid. The number automatically entered can be overridden. It is there to help you save. The same is true for tithing.

Have one column representing each line item in your budget and then another for the actual amount you are spending and earning. Your finished budget or "spending plan" will look something like this. You will have one page for every month of the year. For your convenience, I have provided access on my website to several different spreadsheets that can be used for setting up a budget, in addition to the one I presented in Chapter 9.

The key number to look at here is the balance or a negative number you have at the end of each month. If you have a balance, this is the number you can put toward your long-term savings goals. If it is a negative number, you will know how much you have to cut your expenses by or earn additional income.

If you have the health, time, energy, and desire to work an extra job to increase your wealth, it is an awesome ideology. Extra income can come from many different sources. I have listed a few in Chapter 10 and Chapter 17. Also, you can refer to my website, www.theroadtocreditrepair.com, for a comprehensive list of businesses that can be easily started to generate extra income with a minimal amount of money to start up.

Organizing Your Debt

Now you have a budget. How are you going to pay your bills? The strategy for implementing and carrying out paying according to the budget is considered the process in the IPO strategy.

One of the things that should be a part of the Input section of the IPO is how money from paychecks flows. Do you get paid monthly, every two weeks or weekly? Once you look at how the money comes into the house, break the debt up to best take advantage of paying the bills with the money on hand. For example, if one of the spouses is a teacher who gets paid monthly, his or her check can be used to pay the larger bills or notes—the utilities, car notes, mortgage, insurance, tuition, etc. If the other spouse gets paid twice a month or weekly, his or her check can be used for paying for childcare, groceries, credit card debt, gasoline, etc.

Organizing and assigning a bill to a pay period will remove the worry of how the bill will be paid—and, it brings structure to your overall financial situation.

Build an E.S.C.—an Emergency Stash of Cash

I can't emphasize enough how important it is to put money aside for emergencies. This is how most people get themselves into financial trouble: They keep their heads above water each month, but if there is a surprise major expense or worse yet, a job loss, their well-laid plans start to crumble. I recommend you keep at least three months' worth of living expenses in an interest-bearing account that you can access if needed and this is the bare minimum. Most financial advisors stress striving for six months.

Money markets are a good solution since they pay higher interest rates than a bank's savings account and you can just write a check to use the money. However, the bank will penalize you for more than three withdrawals per month. The exact penalty varies from bank to bank.

Certificates of Deposits (CoD) are inaccessible for the time period you choose, whether it is one year or more. Well, not exactly inaccessible—you can cash in a CoD prior to the maturity date, but the bank will charge you a penalty. One way to use your money in a CoD is to take out a short-term loan against it. This way, it is still intact. The interest you pay on the loan is only about two percent, because there is a two-percent differential between the interest on the borrowed money and that paying on the CoD. If your bank attempts to charge you more than a two-percent differential, go to another bank, but after the CoD matures; otherwise your run the risk of a penalty. After all, the loan they are making is secured and the risk to them is essentially none. If you default on the loan, they will simply keep your CoD.

Start to build up your emergency fund with a few dollars each week and keep adding to it until you reach your three-month (or more) goal. Again, keep it in a money market or some other place you can't get to easily. Make your emergency stash of cash a line item on your budget each month.

Necessities Versus Fluff

Once you've written down everything from the notebook in which you were recording your daily expenditures and you see all your monthly expenses on your budget sheet, take out a big ax and cut! That's right! We're going to cut out the fluff.

First, take a look at your fixed costs. Is there anything here that can be reduced? Here are some ideas:

Cable TV channels. Do you really watch all of them? Could you get a less expensive plan and then ask someone to tape a program for you on a channel you don't receive?

Home mortgage interest rate, home equity loan, and car loans. Frequently check the current rates being offered in the Sunday paper or online. They fluctuate frequently, and you may be able to refinance for a better rate. But beware! *Refinancing is not free.* You will have to pay closing costs; if you do not, it will increase the loan amount on your home. Moreover, refinancing will add time to the mortgage. Before refinancing, be sure to do the MATH.

Watch that thermostat so you are not wasting heat or air conditioning. Adjust the temperature when you are not home or during the night. Visit energy saving websites and implement as many of their inexpensive recommendations that you can. For example, switching to fluorescent lighting will save money on the utility bills, but to purchase the light bulbs is expensive. You will just have to do the MATH to see if it is worth it or not. My opinion is that in the long run, the cost of purchasing the bulbs will be worth it.

Auto insurance. Just by checking around with other insurance companies you may be able to cut your rates. Look at your deductibles and reduce your coverage if your car is getting old. Double up with one company. Some companies offer discounts if they can provide all of your insurance needs: life, auto, and home.

Credit card minimum payments. See if you can transfer a balance to a card with a lower interest rate. Even with a transfer fee, you will probably come out ahead over time. However, beware! Do not open a new card to transfer the balance. We do not want to destroy the work we did raising your credit score. An inquiry on your credit report will have to be made to get that additional credit card—not to mention that the transfer may jeopardize your credit limit to balance owed.

Next, attack your variable costs. If you have been honest, you should be able to see lots of areas to cut here. Try reducing your family entertainment, such as movies and restaurant dining. Take a less-expensive vacation or substitute providing a service to someone instead of gift-giving. Go back to Chapter 6 and check out the list of wasteful spending for some other ideas.

Why Loans and Credit Can Be Your Budget's Friends

There may be times during a particular month that you are caught short of cash to meet all of your expenses. Perhaps the deficit is temporary, until the next paycheck, and you don't want to tap into your savings because you know you will probably never pay it back. I know that you know what this is like.

This is where a home equity line of credit loan could be advantageous. We will talk more about this in Chapter 15 but these loans are basically an amount of money approved by the bank that you can borrow for any reason, any time you like. You just need to make payments on a monthly basis for a percentage of what you borrowed.

These loans will be less costly than reserve credit at a bank, since the interest rate will be much lower. I even found a credit union that offers a home equity line of credit that actually works like reserve credit, in that it kicks in to cover any overdrawn checks. However, you need to be careful with these loans, since your house is being used as collateral. If you have uncontrolled spending habits, you will quickly run up a large balance that you may not be able to pay back on time. Then you risk losing your house.

Instead of using your home for securing a line of credit, if it is short-term, use a CoD as collateral. It is a lot less risky. I have a sincere problem with using the primary residence, the homestead, for securing credit, unless the credit is used to improve the home. Even then, I would have to pray long and hard over leveraging the homestead—even though to reduce our million-dollar debt, my husband and I did just this. Know that was a once–in-a-lifetime activity and that I would never do it again. In other words, we were desperate and had no choice.

If the setback is temporary, use the line of credit on a credit card. Most businesses and utility companies will allow credit card payments. Again, do the MATH. In using the credit card, be sure not to exceed the limit for maintaining a healthy credit score. You may have to use more than one card that you already have to make the payments. Be on your honor to pay the credit card bill as soon as you get the money that you were expecting.

Loans to Avoid

As we have seen, there are a lot of unscrupulous businesses out there who will take advantage of people who are in desperate financial need. I call them "financial opportunists!"

Here are loans you might be able to get quickly and easily but with their high interest charges and inherent risks, they are best to avoid.

Payday loans: Companies who offer these will loan you money based on the amount of your expected paycheck but add a high fee. If you don't pay the complete amount on your next payday, you incur another high fee.

Tax refund advances: Some tax preparation companies offer these, as well as check cashing and other finance companies. The loans are for about ten days and they incur high fees and interest rates. If your tax preparer files online, the turnaround time is very short to get your refund check anyway. Just wait it out! The interest you pay for these types of loans is just not worth it. You should plan carefully what you need to have withheld. There is no point in getting a huge refund when that money could have been sitting in your savings account earning you interest, not in the hands of the IRS.

Pawnshop loans: I can truthfully say that this is something that I never, ever thought of doing when I was in financial trouble because it is the epitome of RIP OFF. Why? A pawnshop owner will advance you a small percentage of the value of an article you bring into the store. If you don't repay the money on time, the pawnshop will sell the item or you will pay a very high interest rate—exorbitantly high. Some pawn shop owners are very unscrupulous. If you miss coming back for your goods by just one day, they will either sell them or charge you more to get them back.

Car title loan: A lender will loan you a percentage of the value of your car and, in addition to high-interest rates, if you miss even one payment, you could lose your car. My thoughts on this rank up there with a pawn shop loan.

Finance company loan: These are smaller, high-interest loans and they may lead you to believe that you don't have to put up any collateral. However, you could risk losing some of your assets if you don't repay them on time, along with their fees. The problem with finance company loans and all the others is that the interest rate entraps and enslaves and all of those other adjectives associated with keeping you paying.

Next, let's take a look at the best type of loan you can get to start building a healthy financial future: a home mortgage loan. Once you get that first home, you can start looking at real estate as a means to build wealth and create income while you sleep.

- CHAPTER 14 -

Mortgages

Credit that will fertilize your money tree.
Credit that will build you wealth.
Saving for it can be fun.
If you dream it, you must believe it.
If you can believe it, you can achieve it.

—Deborah M. Dennis

I know I keep bringing up the fact that there are two kinds of credit—the good and the bad. You know that I believe that credit card spending for frivolous items is the bad kind, because it does nothing to fertilize your money tree. Credit card spending enslaves and you will become a slave to the outrageous interest rates if you cannot pay the debt in full each month.

Interest is what you'll be paying because the repayment structure is orchestrated to keep you paying—and paying interest—not principal. It will take years to pay down the principal of a credit card debt.

Nevertheless, credit is inevitable for some things, like a car that is necessary and a mortgage loan.

One of the best kinds of credit is a real estate mortgage. Although investment in real estate is what landed my husband and me in trouble in the first place, it is also what pulled us through to a positive net— a million net. You don't have to go crazy and become a builder or a flipper (someone who buys old houses, fixes them up, and then re-sells them) to take advantage of all that real estate has to offer.

From the start, I have been telling you that my goal is to start you on the road toward wealth. Now that you have had an opportunity to implement some of the strategies I've demonstrated for improving your credit score, it is time to start looking at building a positive net through real estate. The best way to do this is by first becoming a homeowner.

Let's take a moment to review the benefits of home ownership:

> **You will always have a place to live.** No one can evict you just because the landlord's daughter wants the apartment or the owner doesn't like kids and makes up some excuse. You can paint, decorate, and landscape all to your own personal style. Every time you make an improvement, it only increases the value of your home, to a degree.

> **You will be able to deduct the interest you pay on your mortgage, as well as your property taxes.** In order to en-courage everyone to follow the "American dream" and own a home, Congress has always kept any mortgage in-terest and property taxes you pay as tax-deductible, unless you are at the very high end of the tax brackets. You will be able to have fewer taxes taken out of your paycheck each week, which you can use to pay down other debts.

If you buy in a good neighborhood with good schools (even if you don't have kids), your house will appreciate in value over time. Depending on the area of the country in which you live, this will give you higher returns on your investment than any stock or bond.

If you make your mortgage payments on time each month, creditors will look very favorably upon giving you other loans. The one thing future lenders love to see is that you own your own home and maintain your monthly payments. They see this as stability and you will be viewed as a good credit risk when buying a car or obtaining any other loans.

You can borrow from the equity you build in your home for improvements, college tuition, emergencies, etc. It is not always a good idea to borrow from your house to pay for credit cards or other debts. Studies have shown that after people pay down their cards using their home equity, they drive up their credit card balance all over again and then owe their home equity loan as well as their credit cards. However, if you use it to make improvements, that will increase the value of your house.

Now let's take a look at how you can start the process to achieve you own dream of home ownership. My first suggestion is that you visit my website, www.theroadtocreditrepair.com, and spend some time becoming familiar with the process of becoming a homeowner. This is actually better than attending a homebuyer's training class because of the wealth of information this site provides and you'll be perusing at your convenience. Click on Housing Opportunities.

THE ROAD TO CREDIT REPAIR

Mortgages— A Lien Placed on Property to Secure the Loan Until it is Paid in Full.

In order to become a homeowner, unless you have the cash to purchase real estate, you will need to acquire a mortgage to purchase property.

There are so many programs for first-time home buyers, it is almost impossible to keep track of them all. In fact, the industry went from being very restrictive to completely in favor of the buyer. You could get no verification loans where you wouldn't have to prove your salary or credit history, although the loan would be at a much-higher interest rate. Lenders bent over backwards to provide loans with little or no down payments, as well as interest-only loans where for a few years, your payments would be lower.

However, this has begun to backfire, as people who really couldn't afford the loans they were taking out are now defaulting on their mortgages. The bottom began to fall out of the subprime market around the spring of 2007. The defaults were a factor in bringing down the whole industry as credit began to tighten. Even the builders are finding it harder to get loans for new construction.

When looking for a mortgage, begin at your own bank or credit union. Loyalty has its advantages. They may have a program that works for you. If you need specific information or you need answers to questions that are keeping you from making a decision to become a homeowner, visit my website at www.theroadtocreditrepair.com. There you can find answers to most any question concerning buying a house and obtaining financing.

Mortgage Broker vs. Mortgage Banker vs. Lender

Now that you are interested in becoming a home owner and you are about to begin the search for a mortgage, you need to know from whom you can seek a mortgage. You can obtain a mortgage from one of three sources: a mortgage broker, a mortgage banker, or a lender.

Mortgage brokers represent buyers in their search for a loan to purchase real estate. They have numerous lenders for whom they represent and prepare loans; however, they cannot originate the loan. They do not loan the money directly. Unlike the mortgage broker, the mortgage banker can both originate and resell loans to lenders, such as Fannie Mae or Freddie Mac. The lender is the final step in the mortgage loan process. They are the ones who actually provide the money—cash—for the real estate that you are purchasing. To protect the money that they loan, they attach a lien to the property known as the mortgage.

To help you understand the jargon of the mortgage industry, I provided a glossary of terms and definitions that are commonly used by mortgage brokers, mortgage bankers, and lenders on my website, www.theroadtocreditrepair.com. Becoming familiar with the terminology of the industry can only empower you in your search to find the best loan for your purchase.

In addition to the terms, you should also become familiar with the different loan programs that are available to homebuyers. The HUD website has a wealth of information on the different mortgage types that may be available for you. I provide a brief description of the most popular ones below.

Federal Housing Administration Loans

The Federal Housing and Administration (FHA) does not issue loans directly; rather, it insures the loans lenders make. It is easier to qualify for an FHA loan since you can have a less-than-stellar credit history and you only need to come up with a three-percent down payment. You are allowed to borrow from friends, family, an employer, or charitable organizations, which conventional loans do not allow. Instead of taking out a risky and expensive sub-prime loan, ask about FHA loans at your local bank.

There is a limit on how much money can be borrowed through FHA for a mortgage loan. To find out what the FHA mortgage limit is for your area, visit my website, www.theroadtocreditrepair.com, and click on Housing Opportunities.

Good Neighbor Next Door Program

Designed for law enforcement officers, pre-K–12 teachers, fire fighters and emergency medical technicians to encourage them to live within the communities where they work, the U.S. Department of Housing and Urban Development offers discounts of fifty percent off the price of a home in a targeted revitalization area. In return, you have to commit to living in the house for at least thirty-six months. The number of properties available is limited, but the list changes weekly, so visit my website,www.theroadtocreditrepair.com, and click on Housing Opportunities for more information on this program.

Veterans Administration Loans

If you are a veteran or reservist, or are on active duty, there are many opportunities if you qualify for a VA loan. As part of your military benefits, you can purchase a home under this program without making a down payment. In addition, income, debt, and credit requirements are a little more flexible. To learn more about VA home loan financing, visit my website, www.theroadtocreditrepair.com, and click on Housing Opportunities.

Fannie Mae Programs

These are government-sponsored programs where those with "blemished" credit histories can qualify for loans that could be as much as two percentage points lower than those from traditional lenders. My website, www.theroadtocreditrepair.com, offers prospective home buyers a wealth of information, tools, and resources to help them in their quests. Click on Housing Opportunities to get assistance in finding a mortgage and lender that matches your needs under the Fannie Mae Program.

A Word of Warning

It is never a good idea to take out a mortgage you can't afford. Be very careful of adjustable-rate, interest-only, or balloon mortgages, where your monthly payments will shoot up after a few years.

Also, avoid loans with prepayment penalties. This means that if you have any kind of adjustable-rate mortgage, you won't be able to refinance when the rates go down, if the loan adjusts during the prepayment penalty time frame. You want to be able to take advantage of lower rates, especially if you can convert your current adjustable mortgage to one that is fixed. Hopefully, your income will increase over the years, so it will be nice to know exactly what you will be paying for the next thirty years. Property taxes will continue to rise, however!

If in doubt about a mortgage, or if you need further information on the different types of mortgage loans, visit my website, www.theroadtocreditrepair.com.

Sub-prime Lenders: Going the Way of the Desperate?

There are many mortgage programs for buyers who do not have a lot of money for a down payment, have poor credit histories, or who do not have a lot of income to pay for a large mortgage. Most banks have similar programs. As a matter of fact, if you Google "sub-prime lenders still in business," you will be surprised to find that most are either out of business or ailing in business. However, there are a few around. Just know that if you embark on this road, there is a price to pay: big interest rates.

Sub-prime lending is not all bad. It is good news for those who wouldn't normally qualify for a mortgage loan and have the ability to repay. For example, self-employed individuals, who do not have the financial documentation to prove their income but can cut the payments, could benefit from a sub-prime loan. These loans are bad news if you really can't afford it and having one will put you at risk of losing the house or filing for bankruptcy in the near or distant future.

This will happen with an ARM, particularly because the originator—the one who funded the loan originally, before it was sold in the secondary market—probably did not have their underwriters approve the borrower's ability to repay on the fully indexed rates. This means that the approval was based on the interest rate without any consideration given to the adjusted interest rate.

Sub-prime loans are those that carry a higher interest rate. Sometimes they are an ARM or they may come with a balloon payment (a loan in which the balance of the principal becomes due in full, payable after a certain number of years or months). These loans were given out liberally to borrowers with poor credit histories from 2001 to the early spring of 2007 when they started to decline and now all the problems associated with these loans are coming to light. Many people are facing higher monthly payments that they can't afford, since a lot of the loans were placed as adjustable rate mortgages (ARMs).

Others were written with prepayment penalties and, for a lot of reasons, many loans could not be refinanced for a lower rate. Thus a lot of foreclosures were waiting to happen. The problem was so widespread that the government stepped in to discourage lenders from foreclosing and to encourage them to work out payment arrangements so people could stay in their homes.

One program is called FHA Secure. Believing that some sub-prime borrowers did not fully understand the terms of their loans and are now facing payments that are double or triple what they were originally paying, this program will allow borrowers to refinance their adjustable-rate mortgages—even if they are in default. To qualify, you must have had a good history of on-time payments before your "teaser" rate expired, have at least three percent equity in your home, have a good history of steady employment, and prove you have enough income to make the new mortgage payments.

At the same time, the federal government is looking to tighten standards in lending for home mortgages, and to increase regulations governing banks and mortgage companies. This means that there will be fewer sub-prime loans available and it will not be as easy to get a mortgage loan. Now it will be even more important for you to improve your credit score, pay all your bills on time, and save as much as possible for a down payment. Otherwise, you will still be renting and fertilizing someone else's money tree.

Talk to a Mortgage Lender Early— How to Find a Good One

Before you even start looking for houses, it is a great idea to talk to a mortgage lender and get "pre-qualified." Being pre-qualified means you have an estimate of the amount of money a mortgage lender is willing to loan you in order to purchase a house. If you add that together with what you have saved for a down payment, you have a good idea of how much house you can afford. This can be a great negotiating tool when you go to bid on a house. If sellers know you have already been pre-qualified, they will see you as less of a risk for obtaining financing than someone who has not yet started talking to lenders.

However, before you start looking at houses, find out what property taxes and home insurance will cost and forecast monthly utility bills and condo fees. Ideally, you do not want your housing costs to exceed twenty-eight percent of your monthly income.

Getting pre-qualified is different from being pre-approved. The pre-qualification process only involves the lender obtaining your credit report and an estimate of your income. Pre-approval requires a lot more paperwork as well as verification of all your assets and usually involves a fee. Becoming pre-qualified will be enough to get you started in the negotiating process; however, don't get too comfortable, because it is no guarantee that you will get a loan. You will still need to pass the underwriter's scrutiny.

Always be open and honest with a mortgage lender about your current financial situation. It is a lot easier to get a realistic picture of what you can afford than it is to run into problems further into the buying process. Your credit report and your verified income will give a good picture of your financial status. However, all debt is not reported to the credit bureau and not all income is verifiable. Just remember to be honest with yourself about your financial condition and with the lender. Purchasing a home is a big step. You do not want to get set back before you get started going good.

How Do You Find a Good Mortgage Lender?

Ask friends and family or a real estate broker. Ask them what they liked about working with their lender, and how well that lender explained the process and all their different offerings. Start with your local bank and move on from there. Usually the Sunday paper has a chart showing what the current mortgage rates are for a number of different banks around town. By the time you call on Monday morning, the rates may have changed, but this is a good place to start.

Don't accept the first offer that comes along; look at a variety of mortgage offerings. Check with local lenders as well as those on the Internet. Lenders should also tell you what the estimated closing costs will be, which can run as much as two to seven percent of the loan.

You'll know fairly quickly if you feel comfortable talking with this person and if they are answering all of your questions. If they aren't answering your questions to your satisfaction, take your business elsewhere.

Also, be very careful of mortgage offerings with low rates for the first few years that suddenly spike later on. Unless you intend to get a higher-paying job or come into an inheritance, just beware that if you can't afford those rates today, you probably won't be able to tomorrow. You may be better off waiting another couple of years to apply for a fixed-rate mortgage that you know you can afford.

By studying the answers to the one hundred frequently asked questions about buying a new home that I provide on my website, www.theroadtocreditrepair.com, you can become knowledgeable about the home-buying process and avoid many pitfalls. I highly recommend that you visit my site and spend time becoming familiar with the process.

If you do not have access to the Internet, I suggest taking an adult education class before you start the home-buying process for the first time. Many towns offer inexpensive night classes at a local school and real estate brokers and mortgage companies do as well. You will feel a lot more confident when the professionals start speaking in a jargon containing a lot of unfamiliar terms. The money and headaches you save will more than pay for the class.

Saving for That 20% Down Payment

Of course, there are many mortgage loans you can get that require little or no down payment, provided you have the appropriate credit score. However, your goal should be to keep your monthly payment as low as possible so you do not strap yourself financially with unexpected expenses. Start today by putting an amount to save in your monthly budget; or, better yet, have your employer or bank automatically transfer a set amount each month into your savings account or money market.

Remember that paying rent is a little like throwing money out the window. There is no advantage for you, only the landlord and, specifically, there are no tax deductions. The sooner you can purchase your own home, the sooner you can start building up equity, saving money on income taxes, and building a future for you and your family. Think of your kids and how you want to leave them a foundation.

Another reason to come up with a twenty-percent down payment or more is that you will have to pay for private mortgage insurance (PMI) if you don't. This is insurance lenders take out to protect themselves on the off chance you default on the loan and it can add as much as 0.5 percent to 0.75 percent on top of your interest rate. This will result in an additional amount on top of the normal monthly payment.

I know an individual who pays $284 per month in PMI. He will have to pay this amount until the principal is paid down twenty percent, which gives the lender a twenty-percent equity position. Some lenders will include the mortgage insurance in your interest rate so that you can deduct the full amount on your taxes. You will also be charged a higher interest rate if your down payment is small, so do your best to save as much of a down payment as you can. The other solution is to choose a less expensive house.

Borrowing from Your IRA and Life Insurance

Another way to come up with the down payment is to withdraw up to $10,000 from your IRA account, if you have one. The federal government now allows this for first-time buyers without paying a tax penalty and you don't have to pay it back like a regular loan from your 401(k) plan. However, keep adding to your retirement savings after you buy your house!

One other source of funds is to borrow from the cash value of your whole life insurance policy. You don't have to pay it back, but when you die, the amount is subtracted from the proceeds that go to your family.

Down Payment Assistance Programs

The Department of Housing and Urban Development gives towns and cities money to distribute to low- and moderate-income families, to be used toward down payments for home purchases. This could be as much as a $3,000 to $5,000 grant or a loan that is canceled if you stay in your house for a specific period of time.

However, this is a guideline. The particular city in which you live may be contacted for the award allocated for your area. The award is based on the size of the city and the manner in which the award is distributed also differs from city to city. To qualify, you need to earn less than eighty percent of your region's median income. To find out more, contact your state housing finance authority, the mayor's office, the housing department, or a local community development office.

Pay Down Your Debt

Some experts advise paying down your debt before you put every available penny into saving for a down payment. Even if you end up with less to put down, the interest rates on a credit card are going to be much higher than a home-mortgage interest rate. Most lenders won't grant approval if your debts from credit cards, student loans, car loans, etc. total more than forty percent of your total income.

When Will You Be Ready?

It's hard to pinpoint a particular moment in time when you will automatically be ready to start looking at houses and making offers.

After you have taken an honest look at your current budget and projected earnings, and have met with a mortgage broker for a pre-approval, start looking at houses in your price range only. It is very important to only look at those you can truly afford, as you don't want to fall in love with a home that will bankrupt you in the future.

Look in areas that are commutable to your job. Nothing ruins a day more than sitting in traffic or having to drive an hour or more to and from work. Do your homework and find out which areas have the best schools. Houses in areas with good school systems will always maintain their value. A real estate broker is not allowed to discuss the quality of schools, so look at the school's website and find out the percent of kids going to college and state rankings on standardized tests. Also just ask people who live in the area.

Other things to look for when checking out where to buy a house include:

> The crime rate. The local police station can give you statistics.

> The increase in home values over the past five years. Stop by the local town hall and they can show you their statistics.

> Whether any significant buildings are being planned near your property that will increase or decrease your home value. Does the house border farmland that will turn into a huge shopping center someday soon?

> Whether there are any neighbors who could cause problems. Before making an offer on a house, knock on the door of a neighbor and ask if there are any problems on the street. You don't want barking dogs, trash all over the place, or loud music all the time.

What About Buying Rental Property?

A good way to buy your first home is to consider a multi-family house. The down payment will involve more money, but the rent you'll get from the other units will greatly help to cover your monthly mortgage payments. However, there are several things you should consider before going in this direction:

> Unless you are very careful to whom you rent, you could end up with tenants who are noisy or destructive. It is a long process to evict someone from an apartment, especially if they have children, and even more so if they are savvy when it comes to landlord laws. I once tried to evict a tenant from one of my rentals and she ended up getting an additional month free because the justice of the peace felt sorry for her predicament.

> You could end up with tenants who don't pay their rent on time, endangering your ability to cover your mortgage payments.

> You could open yourself up to lawsuits if you discriminate in any way, such as not renting to people with children or for any rejection based upon color, religion, ethnic group, or sexual orientation.

Plan, Then Stick to Your Plan

Look at your budget to see how much you can put aside each week, determine how much cash you have on hand to come up with a down payment, speak with mortgage brokers, and then come up with a timeline for when you will start looking at houses. If you're not there yet, develop a concrete timetable that states that if you can save X amount per week, either by cutting expenses or increasing your revenue, you will be ready to start the buying process by a particular date.

Put a chart on the wall showing a big gauge of how much you have today in your savings account and the dollar amount of your goal, similar to the chart I provide below. Color in the bar each time you reach a milestone—a savings goal. For example, if the goal is $24,000.00, when you have achieved 20% of the goal, or $4,800.00, color in the bar. Get the family involved in the savings fun. The whole family will see the money growing right before their eyes.

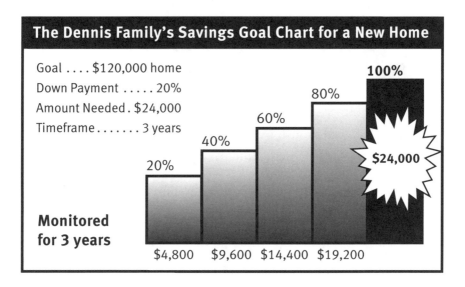

Make owning your own home a plan, not only a dream. Design the planning and the savings to be as much fun as possible. Hold contests to see who can spend less, Mom or Dad. Involve the kids to see who can save the most and make contributions to the goal.

You could even hold fundraisers. It is customary in New Orleans to host dinners—sell dinners—in the neighborhood anytime someone needs to raise money. I've been told that thousands of dollars can be raised from one dinner where the hostess serves fish or chicken, green beans, dirty rice, salad, and cake. However, prior to hosting a dinner, you may want to check with your city first so you do not violate any ordinances or regulations. You can hold a garage sale or make and sell crafts. The trick is to make saving for the goal as much fun as possible—and be sure to involve the kids. It will be their home as well and there is a lesson to be learned from the endeavor. Good luck!

In the next Chapter, we look at ways to use your house like it is your banker.

CHAPTER 15

Using Your House for a Bank—Carefully

When the way is gone,
the light that directs how to get something done will come on,
if you want it bad enough!

— DEBORAH M. DENNIS

The realization of the shape of our finances came when we were faced with paying off a million dollars in debt in less than ten months. Because we were about to lose everything, we realized that a serious change had to take place, which forced a hard look at our financial situation and creditworthiness. This was the only foreseeable way to break the shackles of this bondage. How did we do it? We used whatever we had going for us. We built houses, mortgaged some, flipped others; in all cases, the real estate deals brought in large sums of cash. We manipulated the equity to either pay off or pay down the debt using the IPO strategies presented in Chapters 8 and 9.

Within minutes of the closing of the real estate, the debt was gone. Just like that! Or was it? Actually, in the case where a mortgage was obtained or an equity loan made, it was shifted; or let's just say that it was "Corralled!" We actually cornered it in a place where it could be better managed.

The Truth about Using Equity to Reduce or Eliminate Debt

Before I continue showing you how I used equity in property to eliminate debt, I want to make this point which should be noted: *to take out a home equity loan or extract money from real estate eliminates the debt in one place by shifting it to another.* The debt still exists.

However, there are advantages for shifting debt just like there are disadvantages. What it comes down to is how motivated you are to reduce the debt, how well you understand the consequences of using equity in property to eliminate the debt, and how disciplined you are in "keeping it gone."

When debt is shifted, the note will increase on the property to which the debt is shifted. Because the debt is shifted to real estate that is paid for over a long period of time, the new note should be significantly lower than the combined payments on the debt prior to the reorganization of it. If it is not, then *do not complete the transaction.* If you do, you will probably lose all around.

Debt shifting is a quick fix and if you sell the real estate, it will totally wipe out the debt but only after the real estate is sold or somehow paid in full. Before you take out a home equity loan, perform the necessary diligence to understand what you are about to do. Do not let marketing propaganda, a broker, or anyone who has something to gain from your transaction coerce your decision. Take the time to know and understand what you are doing.

There are significant tax advantages to shifting debt to real estate. If the debt is shifted to a mortgage on a homestead, the principal place of residence, the funds extracted are tax-free, and the interest paid is tax-deductible. The same is true of investment property, as long as the property is rented.

In the case of investment property, not only is the interest tax-deductible, but the principal can be depreciated. Check with your tax professional who can better help you weigh the decision to shift the debt or not to shift the debt.

It is very easy to shift debt and then to create more debt—bad, hollow debt. Please do not fall into this trap. It happens too often to good people. Once you decide to shift the debt, be prepared *to keep it gone* and use the freedom to start developing wealth.

My Story

The complete story of our triumph over our million-dollar debt dilemma was so unbelievable that it inspired a separate book. However, I will give you a synopsis of our success in this section.

I figured out that one of three things would get what was needed to conduct business as a real estate professional: a good credit score (which we didn't have at the time), money (which we had not yet accumulated), and assets (which we had plenty of, but in real estate). Because we were real estate investors, we had property that was loaded with equity. Two of the homes that we'd built had a combined appraisal of about $1 million. We'd built both for less than $400,000. Thus, we had nearly $600,000 in cash that could be tapped from the equity.

However, equity cannot become cash until someone is either willing to purchase your real estate or loan you money using the property as collateral. When you extract money from, or borrow money against real estate, not only is the equity tax-free, but the interest is tax-deductible, provided the property is a homestead or it is rented or leased. In addition, as an investment, the principal can be depreciated—an additional tax advantage.

This worked well for us because prior to this loan, the money we were spending in an attempt to eradicate the debt had no residual benefit. Rolled into the house, the money used to pay the debt was tax-deductible and was being repaid at a much lower interest rate. I personally considered this to be a double whammy.

There are many different philosophies on extracting equity to pay off debt. I encourage you to weigh the odds—and even get professional advice—before extracting equity from your homestead to pay off debt. If you: 1) have the discipline to recognize the benefits of an immediate reduction or elimination of the debt, 2) can make the payments so that the real estate that the debt was shifted to is not jeopardized, and 3) if the value of the property will support the loan, then taking out a home equity loan to reduce your debt is for you. Otherwise, it is not, so *don't do it.*

You are a candidate for a home equity loan if you have:

1. The discipline to recognize the benefits of an immediate reduction of the debt.
2. The means to make the payments, so that your real estate is not at risk.
3. Value in the property that you are refinancing.

First and foremost, it requires discipline to obtain an equity loan to reduce or eliminate debt. We recognized that it was a quick fix for our situation and it was cheaper to pay the interest on the mortgage than it was to pay the exorbitant interest from the hard money lender. Real estate, for us, is a commodity and our ultimate goal is to acquire, hold, and sell at a profit, or to rent or create income while we sleep.

There is no personal or sentimental attachment. It's business!

I had done extensive research on credit repair and I knew that one way to raise the credit score quickly was to keep the debt low on revolving credit cards—around thirty percent of the total debt. We used the money to make this happen, which started us on the road to credit repair.

Everything was going great; then the IRS popped up with a $35,000 tax lien. It's a long story, but I will tell you this: I didn't feel as though I owed the money. However, at the time, we were only disputing $7,000. The IRS felt we owed the money and executed their authority by placing a tax lien on our credit.

After ten years of disputing and negotiation, we gave in and, with interest and penalty, the money had grown to $35,000. This is how much we paid to break free. Are you getting the point? Do not let this happen to you! What we did was plain stupid. If you are ever in this position, don't get tough with the IRS. Trust me—it is cheaper to start paying while you are making your point. This way, at least if you win, you can get a refund. If you lose, the blow won't be as hard.

The fastest way not to get credit is to have an IRS lien showing on your report. I disputed this lien; however, it only dropped from one credit agency. Equifax, the agency most sought by creditors, was not the one; with them, it still reported.

I knew that if we were ever to escape the grasp of the hard money lender—a non-traditional loan shark of a lender—we would have to lose the tax lien. Establishing a payment plan with IRS would get the debt paid over time, but the lien wouldn't fall off until the debt was paid. In other words, it still reported as an unpaid tax lien on the credit report. Therefore, we had to pay the lien in full in order to "silence" its effect.

So we turned to the house again and pulled out the money to pay the IRS. Then we challenged the tax lien and made sure that it was updated as "paid and released" prior to the IRS reporting to the county records department. I sent the credit bureaus my release to ensure that it was updated immediately.

Though a lien stays on a credit report for seven years from the date it was paid, once the lien was paid, the negative impact of an unpaid lien was eliminated. With each passing year, the detriment to the credit score lessens. One more thing: when the lien was paid, I challenged it with the credit reporting agencies. Because the agency reporting the lien—usually the clerk of court in your county—did not update the credit bureaus within the appropriate time period, it was eliminated from the Equifax credit report. The credit score was on the rise again.

The foremost reason why we had to silence the IRS lien was the realization that we were going down fast because of the debt on the subdivision that we had personally guaranteed. The hard money lender for the subdivision decided to call in his note and not loan any more money. Actually, he attempted to throw us into default but an attorney was able to stop him.

Then he cut the funding off totally, which left us handicapped and without any financial backing to complete the project. The complete story on this subject is documented in the book. However, I will tell you this: we were not in default and we never missed a payment to him. We have an order in which we make payments: 1) tithes, 2) insurance, 3) interest (real estate), 4) everything else. Though we were not in default, he held the note and the money, which he cut off. This is when the "way was gone and the lights came on." We had ten months to pay.

In ten months everything would be forfeited if we could not pay the million dollars off and secure release of the deed of trust. All of our assets—blood, sweat and tears; dreams; future; money; life—was in this development. We had exactly ten months to get the hard-money lender paid before the deed of trust came due. If we could not, we would lose everything.

One million dollars! To make a long story short, real estate flipping saved the day. We built and sold—prayed, built and sold. Rain, sleet, or shine, we prayed, built, flipped, and sold. We managed to meet the ten-month deadline through investment savvy, hard work, friendship, and prayer. It's an awesome and inspirational story—be sure to read the book.

We surfaced from that ordeal with a reputation, money in the bank, our credit intact, assets, and a new mindset about the importance of debt reduction and creditworthiness. We vowed never to be in that position again. It was a humbling adventure and it completely transformed our way of thinking about debt and the benefits of having residual income.

We are now landlords, building dormitory housing to rent to students in college towns, as well as to rent to Section 8 clients and others. In the final analysis, we also learned not to depend on one source of income and the importance of generating income while we sleep. In contemporary vernacular, this practice is referred to as having multiple streams of income.

In addition, we build and sell homes via contract for deed, or lease purchase, to people who cannot attain a mortgage but still want to participate in the American dream of homeownership. Amortizing the loan over thirty-years makes for good income and there will be no maintenance on your part because the homeowner has the responsibility for the repairs and insurance. If the homeowner defaults on the loan, because it is a contract for deed, foreclosure is not necessary. You just evict and start the process over with a new buyer. More information on this subject can be obtained from the Road to Credit Repair website www.theroadtocreditrepair.com.

You may wonder how we amassed assets in real estate with bad credit. I am a firm believer that fifty percent of something is better than a hundred percent of nothing. So we borrowed the money from a hard money lender to buy the land and build the houses until we could do better. The interest rate was extremely high; however, the faster you get it done, the less interest you pay. Using a hard money lender as a real estate investor is a valid option. Not all are corrupt. In one of my seminars, "Flip and Create Wealth," I give instruction on how to effectively use the resources of a hard money lender. To find out more information about this seminar, visit www.theroadtocredit repair.com and click on "Seminars."

We worked hard to ensure that the interest we were paying the hard money lender was minimized by flipping the property quickly. The minute I graduated from the school of bad credit, I created financials and a balance sheet and headed straight for the traditional banker's door. We continued to acquire and flip property using money from the traditional lender—building and farming the property in our best interest. Sometimes, we sold and other times we held. We also let our buyers trade their homes for one of ours if the conditions were right for a win-win deal. This provided more assets for our portfolio. Soon the equity in our property, coupled with our monetary assets, was greater than our debt and the difference surged to a million net.

Moreover, we set goals for how much income we would need from real estate to maintain our standard of living, which included taking care of us, my mother, and my daughter, while she attends college. We also wanted to help support our two grandkids—my little gems borrowed from the future that I want to be totally prepared to meet that future when they are reclaimed. To be assured that we would never have to go back to work as an employee, we would need money coming from multiple streams of income. These all were our motivating factors to make sure that money flowed and flowed effortlessly.

Real estate development isn't for everyone. You have to know the business from the ground up, which is usually learned through the school of hard knocks. However, once you have your own home—and I sincerely hope you make this the number-one goal in your financial planning—you can use it to your advantage for future investments or when you are strapped for cash.

Again, I will warn you to be careful of tapping the equity in your home beyond the amount you can afford to pay back. If you do not change your spending habits, you will risk losing your home and that's the last thing you want to risk.

Extracting Equity

Below are two ways to tap into the equity you have built up in your home—which again, is the current value of your home minus what you owe on your mortgage. First, here's an explanation of equity:

$100,000	Original purchase price
- $80,000	Amount you borrowed on your mortgage
$20,000	Amount of equity in your home

Five years later

$125,000	Current value of your house
- $75,000	Balance of your mortgage
$50,000	Amount of equity in your home

It's always a good idea to keep an eye on what houses are selling for in your neighborhood, so you will have a good idea of how much equity you have built up in your home.

Home Equity Loans: Way #1

These are loans where you can refinance your house and have the equity paid to you. In some cases, they are also called second mortgages and allow you to borrow a percentage of the equity you have in your house. In Texas, you cannot tap more than eighty percent of the appraised value of your house in a home equity loan. Another thing, if you live in Texas, once you refinance and extract equity, each time you refinance you will have to take equity out of your home—whether you want to or not. Think about this before you sign on the dotted line.

Home equity loans are very easy to obtain, and in some cases, there are no closing costs.In fact, banks make it a little too easy. These loans are easier to qualify for than a first mortgage if you have less than stellar credit, since the bank will have your house as collateral. (They can take it if you don't pay back the loan.) There are no restrictions on how you use the money.

The good part about using a home equity loan to pay off other debts is that you can usually deduct the interest you pay on the loan—unlike credit card debt, which is not tax-deductible. These loans are generally used more for a large, one-time expense, rather than ongoing financial needs.

A great use of a home equity loan is to make improvements that will increase its value, such as a new kitchen or bathroom. These almost always result in a higher selling price when you decide to sell your house. A poor use of a home equity loan would be a swimming pool or hot tub, since you rarely can recoup your investment when you go to sell your house. An even worse use of a home equity loan is to purchase something that will not grow your money tree, such as a vacation, new clothes, furniture, etc.

Home Equity Line of Credit: Way #2

These loans are a type of revolving credit where you are approved for a specific amount of money that you can borrow and then pay back on an ongoing basis. The amount you will be approved for is based upon the current equity in your home.

These loans can be first or second mortgages, depending on whether or not the home is refinanced. Many people use these if they don't receive regular paychecks. A line of credit lets them cover their bills until they are paid. They usually offer relatively low interest rates and are easier to qualify for than a first mortgage. Again, your house is used as collateral and you need to pay the loan back on time.

Some lines of credit require you to borrow a minimum amount each time, while others make you keep a minimum amount left in the credit line, so shop around. Also, the main difference between a line of credit and a home equity loan is that the interest rate will be variable, not fixed. That means that it could go either up or down over time.

However, by law, lenders must put a cap on the interest rate they charge over the life of the loan. Some home equity lines of credit do allow you to convert from a variable rate to a fixed rate at some point. Some banks may charge for closing costs while some do not, so again, shop around for the best deal.

Reverse Mortgages: An Alternative for Seniors

I know it is difficult to put money away throughout your life for your "golden years." With college tuition, weddings, and ever-increasing property taxes, it's rare to have much money left over to put into savings.

As a retiree, you may be trying to get by on a Social Security check, limited savings, and perhaps a pension, but it is getting harder and harder to cover all your monthly expenses. You start to think you will have to sell the family home and move to a less expensive house or condo. However, before you take this drastic step, you should consider a reverse home mortgage.

Instead of paying the bank each month to pay off your mortgage, the bank will actually pay you. If you have equity in your home, a bank will loan you money that does not have to be paid back until you sell the home, pass away, or permanently move out.

You do not need a minimum income to qualify for a reverse home mortgage. In fact, you don't need any income at all. There are no monthly mortgage payments to make, so you don't have to worry about losing your home through foreclosure.

You must be at least sixty-two years of age and be the official owner of the home in order to qualify for a reverse home mortgage. The amount of money that will be loaned to you depends upon the age of the youngest person who is taking out the reverse mortgage, the appraised value of the home, current interest rates, and the town where the home is located. The older you are, and the more equity you have in your home, the more money you will receive.

Most people prefer to receive the money in a credit line account to use whenever it is needed. Other options include receiving money to pay property taxes and health insurance premiums or even to take a vacation.

Reverse mortgage loans are tax-free and will not affect your Social Security or Medicare benefits. However, if you decide to take a lump sum payment, it is possible that your Medicaid eligibility could be affected. For example, if you take out a reverse mortgage loan of $5,000 to pay off a credit card and have $500 left over at the end of the month, this $500 could be counted as a "resource." If your total liquid resources exceed a particular amount in a given month, you could become ineligible for Medicaid. A Medicaid expert could advise you as to the best course of action to take when you are deciding how much to borrow in a given month.

There are some fees involved with a reverse mortgage loan similar to those you would incur with a regular mortgage. These include origination fees that cover the lender's operating expenses and are currently capped at the greater of $2,000 or two percent of the maximum FHA loan limit. In addition, you will be required to take out mortgage insurance and pay an appraisal fee that ranges between $300 and $400. A service set-aside fee of $30 to 35 per month will also be charged.

You can get the money as a lump sum payment or as a regular monthly check. The funds paid to you from the bank can be used for just about any purpose. You could use it to make needed repairs or home improvements or to pay off credit cards or other debt.

In order to apply for a reverse mortgage, you first have to meet with a counselor. This will be an excellent opportunity for you to ask questions and evaluate alternatives. These might include selling the house, buying a less costly home, moving into an apartment where you would not have to deal with maintenance issues, or moving into an assisted living situation. It is always a great idea to bring a trusted friend, family member, or financial adviser to the counseling session.

Think about how you can be happier and better off financially. However, before you put out that "for sale" sign, certainly consider a reverse home mortgage.

Understand Your Options

Now we have seen that short of becoming a real estate developer or flipper, there are many ways to use real estate to your financial advantage. I hope you agree that home ownership is one of the best investments you can make during your lifetime. If you are not already a home owner, it is imperative that you become one, even if you have to consider the lease purchase or contract for deed route.

Information about these forms of home ownership is on my website at www.theroadtocreditrepair.com. Just be diligent in your decision to go this route, because there are vultures out there who will not have your best interest at heart. You may want to consult a legal professional prior to making a purchase of this nature.

In the next chapter, let's take a look at how working together in the household as a team can bring success as you strive to reach your long-term goals.

CHAPTER 16

It Takes Two to Tango: Working Together Toward Financial Health

The potential for success exceeds the sum of one plus zero.

— DEBORAH M. DENNIS

I'm usually the one who ends up handling all the finances in our family. I have a more flexible schedule, know all the laws, and have great attention to detail. However, this does not mean that I hide things from my husband (okay, maybe once in a while, if I buy something he'll think is frivolous) or that we don't work together to plan for our future.

On the contrary, we work together very closely. Together, we come up with monthly and yearly budgets, and we frequently talk about our long-term goals, such as retirement, supporting elderly parents, investments, and in previous times, saving for our kids' college educations.

You've probably read that money is the number-one issue that couples fight about and it is most likely the main cause of divorce. It is also the main thing people fight about after a divorce. See if any of the following situations apply to your home life and you may recognize some red flags that signal trouble ahead:

> Your husband or wife takes care of all the family finances. If something were to happen to him or her, you would have no idea where your investments are, how much is in the bank, how much money is owed, etc.

> You like to spend money so you pay cash for everything and hide your purchases so they won't show up on a credit card bill.

> You overspend on credit card purchases but volunteer to pay all the bills each month so that your spouse won't be able to question anything.

> When your spouse asks how the family is doing financially, you say, "Just fine," even though you need to borrow every month just to pay the minimum on all your bills.

> You live paycheck to paycheck and never have enough left over to save for unplanned emergencies, insurance, or retirement.

We all can certainly identify with one or more of these scenarios at some point while sharing a household. I believe that the root of money controversy starts with the fact there are two kinds of people in the financial world: spenders and savers. If you are both savers, you will probably have the most peaceful household. Neither of you are extravagant, you both hate to spend money unnecessarily, and you probably have the same goals in life.

Two spenders will not be fighting all the time, but it is much easier to get into debt this way. It is important for spenders to set a budget and develop a savings plan for the future.

On the other hand, if you get a spender and a saver together in a marriage, you may be in for some rocky times. This is more characteristic of my household. I'm the spender and the talker; he's the saver and the worker. Unless you set up a specific plan as to how much you can spend and how much you need to save each month, one spouse may be frequently exasperated with the other's miserliness or over-spending habits. Oh I'm feeling this one!

However, a union of spenders and savers can also have its benefits. I have a friend who made all kinds of money, but hated to part with a dime. He ended up marrying a spender and she taught him how to enjoy life. The next thing we knew, he was buying a beach house and driving a Mercedes.

It was okay, though—they could afford it. If your finances are more limited, a saver can help put the brakes on a spender so that together, you can reach your long-term goals, such as owning your own home, having a comfortable retirement, or putting your kids through college.

Things to Discuss Before You Tie the Knot

It constantly amazes me the things people do not even talk about before they get married. How many times have you heard about couples getting divorced because one wanted to have children and the other did not? This is a basic value and I can't believe the subject never came up when they were dating.

Money also encompasses basic values. Why not discuss them before you tie the knot and avoid a lot of arguments later? Here are some issues that you might want to talk about before you make the commitment to spend your lives together. Perhaps each of you could write your answers down on a piece of paper and then compare responses. Be honest!

What is you personality type? Do you believe in taking personality tests? Why or why not?

How much money do you make? What are your goals for increasing your salary? What is your plan for financial security? Additional schooling?

What is your credit score? What are your plans for improving a bad score? Do you know about an IPO?

Do you write NSF checks? Do you have to have overdraft protection because of your spending patterns?

Do your debts consume your pay checks each pay period? Do you pay your credit cards off each month?

Are you paying child support or alimony? How many kids do you have?

How much do you owe in student loans? Are your loans in default? Forbearance? Deferment?

Do you have a financial planner? If so, how much money are you saving and investing each pay period?

Do you have a CPA? Are you budgeting and reconciling your accounts and budgets monthly?

What are your plans for becoming a wealth builder? Do you believe in working overtime? Entrepreneurship? Landlording?

Would you like to have children? How many? How do you feel about a parent staying home with the kids? How will they be educated?

How do you feel about having separate checking accounts? If you prefer separate checking accounts, how do you feel about the spouse being a signer on the account? How much money can the spouse spend from the account without discussing it first?

Are you a homeowner? Where will we live? When we buy our home, how will we get the downpayment?

Will you sign a pre-nuptial agreement?

Now, there's a hot button—pre-nups! If you are entering a marriage with substantial assets, keep in mind the divorce rate is fifty percent. You may want to protect those assets, but be prepared for some controversy.

If you can answer and discuss all the above questions and still want to marry this person, go for it! You have taken that first important step in communication which is the key to success in managing your finances as a true partnership.

Other Tips for Success

As mentioned above, you will probably want to designate one person to manage all the monthly bill paying. This does not mean that you can hide things and keep your partner in the dark about what is going on. Rather, this person will monitor how much is in the checking account, balance the checkbook each month, and keep track of when bills are due.

Take an afternoon each month and go over your finances with your spouse. Review where you are with your monthly budget, decide what to do with any extra cash, discuss how you are doing meeting your long-term goals, etc. Always keep those lines of communication open!

If one of you has poor spending habits and one of you is a saver, sometimes the best solution is to have separate checking accounts. That's what my husband and I do. If you are both working, you could have three: mine, yours, and the house's. Both of you can contribute to the house account based on a percentage of what each of you earns and after setting aside money for emergencies and long-term plans, you will have the rest to spend as you please.

Allow for some hobbies and other interests. We all have our weaknesses when it comes to spending money. I love to buy clothes for my grandchildren and support charitable endeavors. My husband likes to golf and keep the yard manicured. Total opposites! Notice that shopping or excessive spending is not a part of what he likes to do; yet golfing and yard work can be expensive hobbies. In your household, the hobby may be collecting coins or dolls, scrapbooking, attending rock concerts or sporting events, or whatever. Like a dieter, if you deprive yourselves all the time, you face a greater risk of splurging.

If you have a joint checking account, make sure you set up a reserve credit account. With two people withdrawing cash or running to the grocery store, it is very easy to overdraw and bounce checks. With reserve credit or an overdraft protection account, the bank covers all checks and withdrawals but will charge you a fee for the service. It's well worth it to escape the embarrassment of picking up NSF checks.

If you both are working and have health benefits, one of you may be able to opt out of the company plan and get the money instead. Obviously, choose which family plan has the best coverage and the least cost.

And speaking of work, take advantage of healthcare and dependent care reimbursement accounts if offered by your employer. These are pre-tax dollars put into an account that you can draw from to pay any expenses not covered by insurance. The same goes for paying for daycare. You save money, since your salary is not taxed on what is put into these accounts.

If you have young children, make sure you have a will. This does not have to be a large expense. We got ours done first at an adult education course taught by an attorney. Later as we acquired wealth, I had it revised by my attorney to include more protections.

A will ensures that your assets go where you want them to. However, the main reason to have a will is to select a guardian for your kids in case something happens to both of you. Otherwise, a court of law will have to choose. Knowing who will be raising your children should the unthinkable happen will let you sleep better at night.

Divorce

Let's face the facts—it happens. We all have to keep in the back of our minds that it could happen to anyone.

Divorce brings about financial setbacks for just about everyone involved, but especially women who are usually not the major wage earners. Instead of supporting one household, now there are two with a child support order and/or alimony. You need to be very careful when developing a final divorce agreement since, as we have seen, if you both signed any type of credit agreement, you both are responsible.

Let's say that both names are on your mortgage and that one person is going to continue to live in the house. It may not be a great time to refinance, which is usually the only way to get someone's name off the mortgage loan. What if they don't make the mortgage payments on time? Your credit score will be adversely affected, even though you no longer live there.

The same holds true for credit cards. You need to make sure all past balances are paid and that your name is off the cards. A former spouse could also decide to file for bankruptcy and this notation will be on your credit file for up to ten years, under Chapter 7, if your name is on any of the discharged debts.

An attorney specializing in divorce matters should know how to address all of these issues. It is even more important now to get copies of your credit reports and cancel or freeze any accounts that were jointly opened or for which your former spouse is an authorized user.

You will also be more at risk for identity theft, since your ex knows your Social Security number, etc. You might consider putting in a credit freeze or fraud alert with the three credit bureaus, just to be on the safe side. As I repaired credit for individuals purchasing our homes, there were many instances where this happened. I can tell you horror stories about spouses, both men and women, who disrespected the creditworthiness of the ex-significant other. It takes time, energy, and money to straighten out these messes.

If you are ever involved in a divorce or if you and your spouse are heading for divorce, include a plan to refinance all jointly held real estate notes, decide who is going to keep which card and have the other removed, and close and re-open bank accounts.

Always keep in mind the importance of having a credit history in your own name. If all your assets are in the name of only your spouse, it will be a lot more difficult to get credit in the future. Financial advisers also recommend receiving child support as opposed to alimony, since alimony is taxable, while child support is not.

The other loss many of us may have to face is the death of a spouse. This is why it is so important for the partner who is handling the family finances to share and communicate with the other. The last thing you need in a time of extreme stress is to be left with financial matters you know nothing about.

My husband and I make it a point to keep our attorney informed when we are leaving town, if only through an email, and we make sure that our kids know how to access our financial information, including insurance policies.

On a more cheerful note, let's take a closer look at the long-term savings planning I've been referring to. This will be a great way to fulfill your dreams and to be ready for life's emergencies, large and small.

CHAPTER 17

Saving for a Bright Future

It's funny how the mind can believe what it's told to believe:
If you tell it you have a crop growing, you will.
If you tell it to nourish the crop, it will.
Feed your crop today with preparation for tomorrow.
With the right fertilization,
you'll harvest success in due time.

—DEBORAH M. DENNIS

Sometimes, we need to make sacrifices in the present in order to have a better future. I know that this is hard and some of you may figure, "Hey, I might not even live that long so why should I save money for my retirement?" Others see no need to save for college for their kids, as they think that after high school, they should be ready to stand on their own two feet.

In this chapter, I want to urge you to put some money aside for your golden years and to save for your children's college educations, assuming they want to attend.

Trust me, you do not want to depend on Social Security for all your financial needs when you retire. With all the baby boomers retiring at the same time, the system will be severely strained. There is a good chance that benefits may be cut back or that you will be forced to work for more years than you had planned to. Ask anyone living on Social Security payments today and they will tell you that they feel like they are living close to the poverty level.

Many people are counting on their company pension plans for their retirement years but how often do we read about a company going out of business (think Enron) or suddenly deciding that they are not going to pay health benefits anymore for their retirees? Don't say it could never happen to you!

A college education will help ensure self-sufficiency for your children for the rest of their lives. Do you really want them living at home with you forever, or constantly asking to borrow money? Those with college educations have at least double the earning power, on average, of those who do not. Of course, there are exceptions such as the real estate mogul or the plumber making more than the college professor. A college education or any type of advanced skill training gives one more choices for what they want to do in life.

However, if you have to choose between saving for your retirement or for college, choose retirement. There are no scholarships for retirement, but there are a lot of student aid programs out there. Plus, what you put into a retirement account has all kinds of tax advantages and is not taken into consideration when you go to apply for financial aid.

Next we'll be talking about how to save for both of these important goals, as well as a little about tax planning. A financial planner can also be a great source of advice and we will talk about the pros and cons of using one.

In addition to real estate holdings, long term savings is another method for creating a positive net—and cash is liquid.

Saving for Retirement

Putting money away for your retirement years is one of the best investments you can make and should always be a line item in your budget. The money you invest will multiply over time and you will be able to stop working when you are still young enough to enjoy it.

Most employers offer some type of retirement program and more and more are using 401(k) savings plans rather than traditional pensions. These plans have many benefits, since you can take them with you when you leave a particular job and you don't have to worry about the company not paying the pension should they go out of business or file Chapter 11. Many employers also match what you put into a 401(k) savings plan, so again, it is like throwing money out the window if you don't take advantage of this, no matter what financial condition you are in.

How much money will you need for your retirement? This, of course, depends on how long you will live, but the average person will spend about eighteen years in retirement. Generally, plan on seventy percent of what you are earning now, but if your earnings are low, you will probably need at least ninety percent. If you don't own your home, you will need 100 percent as rent continues to rise.

Your first step should be to get an estimate of what you will be receiving from Social Security, but it is usually about forty percent of what you are now making. You can request an estimate by calling the Social Security Administration at 800-772-1213, or by visiting their website at http://www.socialsecurity.gov.

If you worked for previous employers who offered a pension, you can request an estimate of what your pension will be worth when you retire. Even considering that you may have your house paid off, you will still owe property taxes each year and if you only have Social Security to depend upon, you will most likely come up way short of what you will need to maintain a comfortable standard of living.

Speaking of taxes, be sure that you have the appropriate homestead exemptions filed. Once you reach age sixty-five, you may qualify for another exemption on your homestead. This is true for the disabled as well. Check with your county taxation department to verify whether or not your circumstances qualify you for an additional homestead exemption on your real estate taxes.

The earlier you can start saving, the more money you will have by the time you retire. This is because the interest compounds as the amount of your savings increases. Here is an example:

Jane saves $1,000 every year between the ages of twenty and thirty, totaling $11,000. Then she stops, but she leaves the money in there. Bob doesn't start saving until he is thirty, since he had student loans to pay off, but also invests $1,000 every year until he is sixty-four, totaling $35,000.

At seven percent earnings for both of them, guess who has the most money when they go to retire at age sixty-five? Jane! Due to compound interest, Jane will have saved over $160,000 while Bob will have only about $140,000. So the sooner you can get started, the better.

However, that doesn't mean it is ever too late to start saving for your retirement. Even if you are well into your fifties, you will save more money than waiting for when you are sixty-five.

Under a 401(k) plan (refers to a section of the tax code), you contribute a percentage of your gross income (amount before taxes) each pay period. This amount is then not considered taxable. You will have many choices as to how you want your money to be invested, such as stocks, bonds, money markets, or even company stock. It is a good idea to have a mixture of stocks with more risk along with reliable bonds and money markets. You can change your investment choices, usually quarterly, and can stop contributing at any time.

You will not pay taxes on any interest you earn on these savings until you withdraw it when you retire. Many plans will let you borrow from what you have saved, but if you don't pay it back, there are tax penalties. However, some 401(k) plans do let you withdraw money tax-free to cover a medical emergency or college tuition.

Non-profit organizations' retirement savings plans are known as 403(b) plans. They are similar to 401(k) plans and include tax sheltered annuities as an investment choice.

For those who want to add to their retirement plan at work or do not have an employer-sponsored program, there are individual retirement accounts you can invest in, up to $4,000 per year. If your income is under $110,000 per year, you can invest in a Roth IRA. The difference between these two IRAs is the Roth contributions are made with after-tax dollars, but withdrawals are made tax-free at age 59½. Traditional IRAs are taxed when you withdraw them for your retirement.

If you are self-employed, there are many investment choices. These include a Keough plan, a simplified employment pension (SEP) or a savings incentive match plan for employees of small employers (SIMPLE). Some involve a limit based upon the net earnings of your business, while others do not. It is always a good idea to check with a tax preparation professional before choosing which plan is the best for you.

If you are divorced, make sure you include a provision that you are entitled to a portion of your spouse's retirement benefits, especially if you were the one who left the workforce to raise your kids. This is done using a qualified domestic relations order (QDRO), issued by the divorce court.

One note on investing in cash-value insurance plans for your retirement: this is generally not a good idea, since the premiums you pay are not tax-deductible. You are much better off contributing to a 401(k) plan with your employer or starting your own IRA.

If you want life insurance, take out a term life insurance policy. Because you are building your wealth, my advice is that you at least purchase some form of insurance—maybe a combination of term and whole life. There are many financial planners who can help you create a financial plan. A consultation with one of them can prove to be very beneficial.

Judge Ninfo of the CARE program, which sends out volunteers to talk about money matters with young people, gives a great example of spending versus saving. If your credit card balance is $7,000 at twenty percent interest, you will be paying $116 a month just in interest charges. If you invested that same amount, $116, in a retirement fund, every month from ages twenty-five to sixty-five, you'd have $300,000 in the bank. Which way would you prefer to use your money?

Real Estate Investing and Retirement Planning

I left the security of a stable career when I set out as an entrepreneur. I've told you the story of how hard an adjustment it was for me to change my spending habits. The desire to achieve a goal had to become more intense than the desire to shop in order for me to "quit the habit." When I did, I vowed never to go back to that way of living—paycheck to paycheck, project to project. I wanted money flowing all the time, even as I slept.

The truth is that with the economy growing annually, when you retire, unless you plan carefully, you will eventually fall below the poverty line. On a fixed income, it will be difficult to stay above the line and maintain some of your pre-retirement lifestyle without a substantial nest egg. Check with a financial planner if you don't believe me.

Thus my husband and I had to put into motion a plan to keep this from happening to us. How did we do it? We generated residual income through real estate investments. I call the ability to make money as you sleep generation of residual income. We generate this income through rentals and dorm houses.

Dorm houses are houses that we build to rent in college towns, where student enrollment creates a need for off-campus housing. We look for towns where the prospect for the college to remain solvent is indefinite. Then we buy land, build dorms, and rent them to the students wanting to live off-campus. It's another stream of income, a great one. Because the dorms are new, they don't require too much maintenance. We have the parents of the students personally guarantee the leases, so we know that payment will not be an issue. The money is good and it is a great form of retirement income.

This works for us. I encourage you to think of some ways that you can generate money while you sleep. Later in this chapter, I discuss network marketing as a part-time business. There are two that we participate in as associates: BookWise and Tahitian Noni Juice. A network marketing business can prove to be an excellent home-based business and a perfect way to earn money while you sleep. If you are adamant about saving for your kids' college, BookWise is the perfect answer.

Saving for College

Today's college students are already spending upwards of $180,000 for four-year degrees at private institutions. Sure, you can find state schools for a lot less, but everyone else has the same idea and sometimes they are hard to get into. With tuition prices rising at about eight percent each year, a child who is four years old today will easily be spending well over $250,000 by the time they graduate.

The good news is this: if you start saving when your children are youngsters, your money will quickly multiply over the years—assuming you are smart with your investments. Again, get a good financial advisor who can help you plan for your children's future. If you invest just $100 a month for eighteen years at eight percent interest, you will have $48,000 to spend for their first year of college. This is a minimum. If you invest wisely, the return may even be greater.

Most colleges, and the federal government, offer some form of grants and aid and there are also lots of private scholarships available. Parents should expect to pay at least one half to two thirds of the total cost and more if you are in a high income bracket. So starting to save the day the child is born will generate as much interest on your money as possible, lessening the amount you will have to borrow later. It is always better to earn interest on your money rather than paying it for a loan. However, you do need to try to avoid saddling your child with a lot of debt that will take years to pay off.

Several factors go into determining how much financial aid you will qualify for. These include your income, your non-retirement assets, such as how much equity you have in your home, how many other children you have, and the student's income and assets. Obviously, it is much better to get scholarships and grants than loans, since you won't have to pay them back.

One federal program is the Pell Grant, given primarily to low-income families, which offers up to $5,000 depending on need. There is also the federal Supplemental Educational Opportunity Grant which is administered by the colleges. These are also need-based and students are expected to work in a work-study program as well. If you are applying for these, be sure to file early and provide the colleges with the results as soon as they come in. The early bird gets the worm when it comes to college financial aid and subsidy.

These days most families are depending on loans to fill the gap between what they can afford and what tuition costs. If you are a middle-class family, the odds of you getting a grant are slim to none. This is reserved for the family who meets the criteria for being at risk of poverty.

Some of the most attractive loans are need-based as well. These include the federally-funded Perkins and Stafford loans. Perkins loans are made directly to students who don't have to start paying them back until nine months after they graduate. They have ten years to pay back a Perkins loan and the interest rate is usually around five percent. The interest rate for a Stafford loan is variable, but capped around 8.25 percent.

There are also non-need-based loans, such as the unsubsidized Stafford and a PLUS loan, which stands for "parent loans for under-graduate students." PLUS loans are made to the parents, not the students and are dependent on a good credit rating. However the standards are not as strict as they are when you're qualifying for a mortgage. The interest rate is variable and you must start repaying it sixty days after you receive it. You also have ten years to repay it. Also, be sure to look into Signature Student Loans, offered by the federal program Sallie Mae, and Excel Loans from Nellie Mae.

Many people believe they should keep most of their college savings in the child's name, since they are in a lower tax bracket. Nothing could be further from the truth. When colleges put together all their formulas to decide how much they think you can afford to pay, they assess what the student has saved at thirty-five percent and what the parents' assets are at 5.65 percent. You have a better chance of getting financial aid if most of your savings are in your name.

The best place to save for college is in stocks or mutual funds. Sure there will be large dips in earnings at times, but over many years you will earn more than any other type of investment (except maybe the right real estate). Like retirement savings, the trick is to convert them to a more conservative type of investment, such as bonds and money markets, as your child gets closer to graduating from high school.

State-sponsored 529 savings plans are a great way to save for college. You can save between $100,000 and $270,000 per child and when you withdraw the money to pay for college, it is tax-free. There are no income limitations or age restrictions and you can save as much as $270,000. Like a retirement account, you get to choose how the money is invested in various stock and bond funds, and the fund will invest more in stocks in the early years and more in bonds as the child gets older.

You can get a credit card through a bank or investment company where one percent of whatever you spend goes directly into a 529 savings plan. In addition, there are loyalty programs such as U-promise, BabyMint, and SAGE Tuition Rewards. If you register with them, every time you shop at a particular store or pay for certain utilities, a percent will go toward your college savings.

In addition, you will hear about state-sponsored prepaid college plans. This is where you can pay now at today's tuition rates, for a college education tomorrow in your particular state. However, these do not include the cost of room and board and there is a possibility your child may not want to go to school in your state, so you would lose some of the fund's value. Experts believe a 529 savings plan has many more benefits than a prepaid plan.

Tapping into the equity in your home is another way to help pay for college, which is another reason not to keep using it to pay off credit cards and other debts. You can also borrow from your retirement fund, such as a 401(k), but will have to pay it back or incur huge tax penalties.

Perhaps the only piece of good news about paying for college is that you can get tax credits, such as the Hope and the Lifetime Learning credits for the years in which you are paying college tuition. You might also be able to deduct the amount of interest you are paying, depending on your income level.

Read Your Child Into College

In my family, it is imperative that you graduate high school and attend college. Not only is it expected, it is mandated. No arguments accepted! You may look upon this as meddling or being mean; I look upon it as a necessity. You see, I feel that our kids are loaned to us from the future. As parents, it is our responsibility to give them back as best-prepared as possible.

As baby boomers, we enjoyed many opportunities that do not exist for our kids. Competition is greater. Living in this information age, an age of automation and advanced computer literacy, we find that a lot of the jobs that we once performed are being performed by robots, outsourced to Asia, or with much less personnel. What I am trying to say is this: the workplace is more competitive and our kids need all of the tools that they can gather to help them compete. It does not matter what race, religion, or sex one is. To be successful in the workplace, you had better be prepared to compete.

Having made the argument that college is essential in today's economy, a family may find it difficult to put money aside for college. Good intentions spring into action, but then the money has to be used to make ends meet. Let me make a suggestion: Let your kids read their way into college by establishing a book club for them.

As parents, we have to circumvent the hold that the computer age has on our kids. It takes a village to raise a child these days. Thus, MiMi—that's me—decided to shore the concept that reading is FUN-damental—with emphasis on the FUN. I bought my grandkids a bookstore through an organization called BookWise. I set up their personal book club with me as the owner. An adult has to be the owner.

The plan is for them to invite several of their friends to participate. There will be a nominal membership fee to join and each month the members receive a book to read. A certain number of days will be allotted to read the book. The book will be discussed at a party once a month. Your kids will enjoy this tremendously and it is good clean fun, which will develop a love for reading in the process.

Accompanying the membership is both a website and a bookstore that anyone on the Internet can access and buy from. The books are purchased from BookWise at a discounted price, and they are sold to the members at the retail price. For example, let's say that my grandson buys the book of the month from BookWise for $14.00. He, in turn, sells the book for $20 (or whatever the retail value is). If he has ten kids in the club, then he makes $60 from selling the books. In addition, if a kid in the club wants to start a book club, he will be entered under the down line for our book club. Money is earned from this as well.

Are you wondering how this can be used to start a college savings? All of the proceeds from the books sold to the members and any commission earned through new member sign–ups, are sent to a mutual fund. This money is invested and saved for college. Not only is the book club enriching, it is a productive, fun, and safe way to visit with friends; and the kids earn money for college while they are learning and having fun. When the kids become old enough, they can take over the management of the business.

BookWise is a company that was founded by Robert Allen, bestselling author of Nothing Down and several books on real estate investing, and Richard Paul Evans, bestselling author of *The Christmas Box*. BookWise is the most intelligent home-based business in the world. There is a small monthly fee to maintain membership, but the fee, in comparison to the support the company gives, is minimal.

I invite you to visit my website, http://www.mybookwise.com/gemsoftomorrow/ and check out the many advantages of owning a BookWise bookstore. If you want to learn even more about Book-Wise, go to http://www.winninginthemargins.com and listen to the presentation by one of the founders, Richard Paul Evans. You can use my passcode to enter the site: ***readingisfun.*** If you see the benefit in it, sign up. Once you become an associate, I will be assigned as your sponsor and you can begin your college savings as well as the fun and enjoyment of wholesome reading with your kids.

Some of the BookWise Benefits

A BookWise home-based business comes with a twelve-month, one-hundred-percent-satisfaction, money-back guarantee! What this means is that after the first year, if you are not completely satisfied with your bookstore for any reason, you can request a refund of the money you invested. In addition to this guarantee, as an associate, you get the following monthly:

A hardcover bestseller

An e-book

An audio book

Forty to fifty percent off retail

Weekly WealthWise training

Two tickets to the AuthorWise Writers Conference

A speed-reading lesson

A monthly newsletter

Weekly author Webcasts

Monthly TaxWise training

The benefits of being a BookWise associate, listed above, are explained in depth during the Richard Paul Evans presentation. Again, go to http://www.winninginthemargins.com and listen to the presentation by Richard Paul Evans. You can use my passcode to enter the site: *readingisfun.*

Besides real estate investing and BookWise, we participate in a network marketing business called Tahitian Noni Juice. Visit my website, www.tahitiannoni.com/deborahdennis, for more information on this business. You can also link to this site and BookWise from the www.theroadtocreditrepair.com website.

If you are looking for a small business to work from your home that is both rewarding and beneficial, I highly recommend BookWise and/or Tahitian Noni. For supportive information on how to successfully run a home-based, network marketing business, visit www.theroadtocreditrepair.com. Once inside, click on the category for a home based business and then select network marketing. There is a mountain of information `on Multi-Level Marketing strategies as well as suggestions for reading.

The one thing to always keep in mind in order for any business to be successful, no matter what kind, is this: two fundamental things must happen. One, the business has to be funded; and two, it has to be worked. I offered these two businesses because of the low cost each month to maintain membership as well as the benefits of the product. For much less than a $300 investment per month, there is the potential to earn a five figure monthly income. The value of the products and the compensation structure make both a candidate for a viable in-home business.

Seven Feasible Reasons for Starting a Home-based Business

1. You are in complete control of how much money you make on a weekly basis. You can make as little or as much money as you choose. The more money you want to earn, the harder you will have to work to acquire it. Your fate is in your control.

2. You have the complete power to make things happen according to your choosing. You have the ability to work as hard for you as you currently work for someone else and you can keep all of the profits that you generate. You are your sole supervisor.

3. If you choose to start a home-based business as a part-time job, you can conduct this part-time job from the comfort of your home. And you can make as much money as you need per your own schedule. The control is one hundred percent yours.

4. You do not have to punch a clock so you will be in control of setting your own work schedule. Because you will be working from home, you can schedule your time around PTA, establish a school volunteer schedule, have meals prepared on time, better handle the kids' extra-curricular activities, meet during the day with friends for lunch, bridge, or shopping, or even take a nap if you are tired.

5. The life you live will be greatly enhanced. If the business that you choose is Internet-based, you have the flexibility to work from anywhere in the world: either on vacation, from a hotel room, in Las Vegas, on a cruise, in the airport, or in the car. Anywhere that you have the ability to establish an Internet connection, you can work. You will be set free to either work and play or work and bond with the family simultaneously.

6. Because you will be your own boss, you will have job security. Never again will you be subjected to the fear of losing your job because of a corporate buyout or company downsize. You will never be humiliated by a boss who has you training someone to take over your job.

7. You can start living your dreams and accomplishing the goals that you set for your personal growth, livelihood, and family. The sky will be the limit as you operate with the freedom to dream dreams and implement them per your own choosing.

How Much Tax to Withhold

Tax withholding can require a delicate balancing act to come up with the right amount. On the one hand, you do not want to have too much withheld and then get a huge refund every spring. Some people like to do this, since it is forced savings for them and they can pay down credit cards, etc. However, as we previously discussed, you are losing out on a lot of interest and your use of the money.

On the other hand, having too little withheld will result in unnecessary tax penalties and you will have to scramble to come up with the money. There goes your emergency stash of cash again. If you have outside income in addition to your regular job, you should withhold more money at work or pay estimated quarterly tax payments to the state and federal governments.

Keep in mind that local, state, and federal taxes cannot be discharged under a bankruptcy filing, nor can you have credit card charges eliminated that were used to pay your taxes. It is a good idea to meet with a tax planner once a year to review what you are currently withholding and determine if any adjustments should be made. And remember, one of the best ways to pay fewer taxes is to contribute as much as you can to a retirement account!

Budget Booster: Saving on Taxes

If you've always prepared your own taxes, you may not be aware of many deductions you can take to reduce your tax bill. This is especially true if you have any kind of at-home business. Here are just a few areas to look at if you are not already taking advantage of these provisions:

> You may qualify to itemize your deductions. This is done on Schedule A. Add up all the deductions you can take, which include medical expenses, other taxes you pay, interest payments on a mortgage, charitable deductions,

unreimbursed employment expenses, etc. Then compare them with the standard deduction you would get if you were not itemizing on Schedule A and choose the greater of the two.

For your home mortgage, don't forget to include points you paid at closing, if you purchased a home or refinanced during the tax year. Other closing costs may be deductible as well. Points paid for refinancing must be amortized over the life of the loan.

If you make your January mortgage payment in December, you will have an extra month's interest payment to deduct.

For charitable deductions, you can include donations of clothing or household goods. The IRS has guidelines as to the value of each type of item. Always keep a receipt or a canceled check for your records and try to pay by check for all your donations, including what you give to your church.

You can deduct some of the fee you pay to register and license your car.

Educational expenses are deductible, including tuition, books, and travel costs to and from classes, if they are related to your current career. If they are to learn a new career, they are not deductible. You can also deduct legitimate costs relating to finding a new job within your field, including travel and career counseling.

Unreimbursed expenses that are related to your current job include training classes, magazine subscriptions, books, a special chair you require for medical reasons, a uniform and the cost of cleaning it, union dues, and membership fees in a professional organization; these are all deductible. A computer can also be deducted if it is used outside your office but only if these three conditions are met: it's for the convenience of your employer, is a condition of your employment, and is used more than half the time for business purposes.

Tax preparation fees, investment and tax advisory fees, and subscriptions to investment and tax-related publications are deductible.

In addition to the above, if you have any kind of self-employment income aside from your full-time job, make sure you are taking advantage of these deductions:

Computer equipment and other large purchases, which are depreciated over a period of time

Advertising

Travel expenses, including mileage (keep a notebook in your car)

Parking, tolls

Bad debts, uncollectable bills

Insurance

Legal and professional services

Office expenses and supplies

Rent or lease payments

Repairs and maintenance

Taxes and licenses

Phone and Internet bills

Utilities

Cost of hiring your children to do work for you

Dues and subscriptions

Mailing costs

Professional development courses

Amount you contribute to a retirement plan

Entertaining clients (a reasonable amount)

Hopefully, the next time you prepare your taxes, you will come up with additional ways to cut your annual tax bill. In most cases, you need to make a profit from your business for three consecutive years out of five or the IRS will consider it a hobby, not a business, and disallow everything. Consult with your tax preparer or seek advice from a CPA on deducting a home office as well as for obtaining professional advice on how to save on taxes. The IRS tax code is complicated, and a professional can help you maximum your deductions.

I cannot emphasize strongly enough the importance of keeping good records and getting receipts for everything. This will make it so much easier at tax preparation time and you will be well-prepared if, by chance, you are ever audited.

Hiring a Financial Planner

You don't have to be rich to hire a financial planner—someone who is there to help people from all walks of life manage their finances, invest for the future, and pay the minimum amount of taxes. There are two types of financial planners: fee-only and commission-based. Always check to be sure that they are certified before doing any business with them.

Planners who are commission-based do not charge hourly fees for their services. Rather, they take a percentage of the investments they sell you, whether it's an IRA, a mutual fund or a particular stock.

Fee-only financial planners will charge hourly fees for their services, which could run $30 per hour on up but will be totally unbiased when they recommend certain investments. You can get financial planning services for free, but be prepared for a hard sell to purchase their products and services.

A good financial planner can help you choose investments to save for your retirement or college and advise you on how to shelter your earnings from taxes as much as possible. Perhaps you received an inheritance and are wondering how to invest it, or you are self-employed and need to set up an IRA. They can also advise you on what insurance you should have, including life, disability, and long-term care.

In addition to being certified, ask your planner if he or she has any professional designations, such as the chartered life underwriter (CLU), chartered financial consultant (ChFC), certified financial planner (CFP), or certified public accountant (CPA). Then you will know that he or she is keeping up on all the latest information and has the highest professional standards.

CHAPTER 18

Give Yourself Credit!

From the withered tree,
a flower has bloomed.

— CONFUCIUS

Now you are coming to the end of your credit repair journey. You have come such a long way in your quest to learn how to improve your credit score, reduce your debt, and budget to control spending, as well as how you can use a house to your advantage. This is a lot of information to absorb, so you may want to prioritize what to address first as you continue along the road to credit repair and debt reduction. Congratulations! You are on your way and I wish you the best in the future.

Going forward, here are my suggestions to keep you successful:

Send for your credit report to see if your fixes worked and correct any errors still existing.

Set up a reserve credit account for emergencies and establish automatic bill payments with your bank or credit union. Resolve never to bounce a check or pay a bill late. If you ever get in the predicament of having to pay a bill late, be conscious of your credit score and make the payments prior to the next due date so that your payment is not thirty days past due.

Develop a family budget that includes all yearly and monthly expenses. Try very hard not to go over your budgeted amounts, unless you subtract it from something else. Strive to keep a balance between what you want and what you can afford.

If you cannot meet your monthly budget expenses or set aside money to save for your retirement, house, college, etc., make a plan to increase your revenue.

Make sure you carry the minimum amount of health insurance for you and your family. (More on this in a minute.)

If you don't already own your house or condo, make a concrete plan to buy one within a specific period of time.

If you can't do most of the above on your own, don't hesitate to seek help from a licensed credit counseling service.

Be a Positive Thinker!

You will face some dark days when financial health seems way beyond your grasp. Your car or house will need some major repair (there goes your emergency stash of cash); your child may need braces or you may lose your job. However, keep up the positive thinking that motivated you to start on the road to credit repair. Depend on it while you weather each and every storm and you will eventually get back on track.

As you read my story, either the part that was exposed in this book or the whole story in my book, *In God We Trust—The Mindset of a Successful Real Estate Investor,* you will see that we overcame our adversity because we kept a positive attitude. Time after time, adversity reared its ugly head and time after time, we overcame it because we focused our eyes on the goal, the dream—not the problems at hand.

It is possible to realize your dreams, but it will take a certain amount of sacrifice from the entire family. Prioritize, scrutinize, and analyze your finances at least a few minutes every day! With online banking, this is very easy to do. I cannot express enough the value of a budget when you are trying to build wealth and the value of a plan.

When your credit is healthy and your outlook is bright, give yourself honors for this accomplishment and splurge on a big peace of mind. It is very easy to backslide into old spending habits, especially when you see all those nice credit cards sitting there with zero balances. When new ones come in the mail, shred them—don't even open the envelopes. You do not need, nor do you want, the temptation.

I keep a shredder at the place where I open the mail. I shred junk mail before it gets into the house good. I classify unsolicited credit card applications as junk mail. Remember, if you are not in a position to pay your credit card purchases in full at the end of the month, don't CHARGE. If your credit card purchase will not fertilize your money tree, don't buy on credit. PERIOD!

You can cut up most of your cards without officially canceling them, saving one gas card, one department store card, and one major credit card that can be used anywhere. If you have to choose, pick one that either gives you cash or airline points or one that contributes a percentage to a 529B plan for college savings. And for goodness' sake, again, pay them off each month!

If you have to, set a limit in your budget as to how much you can afford each month on credit cards. Keep a notebook with you to record every time you make a credit purchase. Once you hit that point, quit buying until the next month. I have held up lines at cashiers to record, in a simple checkbook log, the credit card purchase I just made.

Especially if you are using your debit card, develop this discipline because debit card purchases are not charge card purchases. It is easy to forget that they are deducted from your checking account. You do not want to run the risk of paying overdrafts and NSF charges. Now banks hit you double. They charge you for an NSF fee as well as for overdrawing the account if the balance goes negative. Can you believe it?

When your credit score is well above 700, you can very slowly cancel the cards you won't need anymore, about one every other month. That way, your available credit versus what credit you've used will remain high. Just remember that to have a healthy credit score, you only need three types of credit: real estate, installment, and revolving. Once the credit scoring model detects that you are a responsible, creditworthy individual, you can downsize your available credit to only one of the three types.

The key is to always be cognizant of how credit works. The limit is not as important as the ratio of the balance to the limit. Thus you can have a $500 limit with a $150 balance and be in great shape. This is manageable. Though paid-in-full installment debt loses its potency after two to three years, if you decide to revamp this debt, buy within your means. Moreover, try to make installment purchases that will empower you, like a car or business tools. Though they lose value, they fertilize the money tree by providing opportunities for you to make money.

Rule of thumb in the Dennis household: we never finance cars for more than three years and we never have more than one car loan at a time. We buy brand new, conduct scheduled maintenance, and drive them until they just won't go anymore. We never buy without a down payment because the goal is to pay the car off in three years.

I am a firm believer, as you know, that real estate investing will keep your lifestyle comfortable. Be smart about your real estate investing, but once your credit score improves and debt is reduced, do buy real estate and hold on to it.

In the spring of 2007, the bottom started to fall from under the sub-prime market which caused a tremendous amount of real estate to be available at great deals. In markets like this, it is an awesome time to buy and hold. All of those homeowners who lost their homes will have to stay somewhere. Unfortunately, when the bank foreclosed, their credit took a dive. Thus they are prime candidates to rent. If you offer a clean, quality home, you will have a renter for a few years. If your intention is to sell after the market corrects, you may even have a built-in buyer. Moving is a pain and the renter may very well opt to stay.

I have consulted many lenders on how many real estate notes can report on the credit report. The one consistent response is that the lender looks at the ability to repay and the amount of equity in the home. If the rentals are cash flowing (that is, if you have it rented and are making money from the rent), then how many is not important. The formula we use is never to buy or build real estate to rent where the loan-to-value ratio exceeds more than seventy percent. Thus we always have thirty percent plus equity in the home, which is good if you have to unload it in a hurry.

In the future, I will be writing a book on the subject of buying and farming real estate. In addition, I will be offering coaching and seminars to show you exactly how to do it. Some coaches only tell you what to do; on the contrary, I will be telling and demonstrating, through hands-on coaching, how to stand on your own two feet as a real estate investor. Not only will I tell you what to do, but I will show you just how to do it and where to go to get the money. There are many ways to buy real estate without using your personal credit and money. If you are interested, send an email to deborah@theroadtocreditrepair.com and I will notify you when the book hits the market.

How to Avoid Backsliding

Research has shown that it takes a minimum of three months to change any type of bad habit, so don't expect a magic change in your spending behavior overnight. You will have temporary setbacks, but that does not mean you should give up on saving and lowering your amount of debt. Just get back in the saddle and start over!

Set short-term goals for yourself, such as packing a lunch instead of going out and later, giving up the fancy lattes. This is a marathon you are running, not a 100-yard dash. If you have a friend with the same goals, challenge and help each other throughout the process. Here are some other tips to avoid backsliding:

> Set small, achievable goals. Instead of planning to put $5,000 into a retirement savings plan this year, strive for $100 per week.

> Stay away from the places where you like to spend money. This could be the mall, a coffee shop, a hardware store, sporting events, etc. Try catalog shopping when you need something specific. It eliminates unnecessary temptation.

> Have money go directly to a savings account or money

market from your paycheck. That way, you won't be tempted to use it for other things.

Always keep your end goal in focus. If you are saving for a house, go to open houses, and look online and in newspaper ads. That might help you keep on track when you are tempted to stray.

Use your debit card instead of a credit card. Debit cards purchases are cash purchases. You won't be able to use it if the money is not in the bank, unlike a credit card. Be aware that some companies put a hold on a checking account for much more than the purchase amount until the funds clear the account. This will leave you with less available cash and it may cause other checks to bounce. Just beware when using your debit card, especially for gas and car rentals and at restaurants.

Budget Busters: Medical bills

While repairing credit for clients buying my homes, I noticed that outstanding debt on medical bills was killing their credit scores. It used to be that the medical profession was not aggressive in putting debt onto the credit report. However, that changed when mortgage loans became a commodity. They realized that the debt would have to be paid or settled before a mortgage loan would be granted. Thus, more and more, you see this debt popping up on credit reports.

Studies have shown that fifty percent of all bankruptcies are filed due to unmanageable medical bills. In a country as wealthy as ours, we need to find a way to make sure that no one loses all of his or her assets due to a medical crisis. Next we'll look at some ways to ensure this doesn't happen to you.

Catastrophic Insurance

Personally, I would not get out of bed in the morning without health insurance. With so many crazy drivers out there and the "fickle finger of fate," which can randomly choose us to come down with serious illnesses, it is just not worth the risk.

If you can't get health insurance through your employer, shame on them. You need to buy the minimum amount of insurance to at least cover hospitalization. It is very expensive to purchase this on your own, so try to find a group plan to buy from. Just about every professional organization offers one—the Chamber of Commerce, small business owners, unions, teacher organizations, self-employed businesspeople, truck drivers, you name it. You will probably need to join the organization first, at a nominal cost.

If you meet certain income requirements, you could qualify for Medicaid or other plans offered by your state or the federal government, for those who can't afford health insurance. Go to http://www.cms.hhs.gov/medicaid/stateplans to find out about your state's Medicaid program.

If you are self-employed, I highly recommend disability insurance, especially if you are the major breadwinner in your household. If you are disabled and can no longer work, insurance will pay a percentage of your past earnings. Think about how your family would survive without it.

Term life insurance is also a good idea if you are the only one employed in your family, for the same reasons. And if you have the money to spare, long-term care insurance is a great idea. You will be able to have a choice as to which assisted living or nursing home you would go to and it will also pay for in-home health care and other services.

Is Your Health Plan Paying What It Should?

Health plans in general are notorious for denying claims or just procrastinating on paying the medical bills that they are supposed to cover. I wish I had a dime for all the hours I've spent on the phone, chasing down my insurer and constantly bugging them to pay my medical bills. It could literally be a full-time job. Even after they are fined and penalized for giving their members the run-around, they still do it.

Don't let them get away with it! I switched carriers. Fortunately, I was able to join a group plan through the Chamber of Commerce. Now, my carrier is a lot better about paying; however, the premium is competing with a rocketship to the moon.

Know what your plan covers; get your employer involved if you have company health insurance and call every day if you have to. Insurance companies are literally banking on people giving up and paying out of their own pockets, rather than forcing the companies to pay what they are supposed to. If you are denied a claim that you firmly believe they should pay, file an appeal. If that doesn't do the trick, report them to the state insurance commissioner's office, as they may be of some help. If all else fails and a large amount of money is at stake, hire an attorney who will work on a contingency basis, meaning they take a percentage of whatever they win for you.

The important thing is not to give up. If you don't pay your medical provider, they will most probably scar your credit. So, don't ignore those medical bills. Pay your co-pays, work out payment plans when your portion of the bill cannot be paid in full, and by all means, do not ignore medical bills that come in the mail. By doing so, you will set yourself up for failure.

Get a Discount

You may not be aware that insurance companies pay far less for medical services than you or I do if we are uninsured. I am talking about the exact same doctor performing the exact same service.

If you have large medical bills to pay and do not have health insurance, always ask for a discount. If you offer to pay the full amount upfront, they should be more than willing to discount it at least forty percent. If you don't have the money, check out the hospital's programs for free medical care for those who can't afford to pay. If you make too much income to qualify for that, stretch out the payments as much as you can.

Remember that late payments for medical bills do not show up on your credit report. However, non-payments do. Even if you can only pay $20 per week, they will see that you are trying and will hopefully leave you alone. If they don't, and threaten to sue, tell them you will be forced to file for bankruptcy and they will likely end up with nothing.

Another Budget Buster: Student Loans

It is so sad to see young people graduate from great colleges, after majoring in professions they have always dreamed about, just to be saddled with thousands and thousands of dollars in student loans. What's really sad is if they end up working in professions that don't pay well.

Medical school or law school is one thing, since there is the potential to make good money. However, take the job of university professor, where it is almost a requirement that you have a Ph.D. That's at least eight years of college, with not a lot of earning potential. I have no idea how students graduating with all these loans will ever buy houses or save for their own retirements.

We touched a little on how you can be excused from your student loans if you are really indigent, but what if you have a halfway decent job and this doesn't apply to you? Even if you file for bankruptcy, there are certain types of loans that cannot be discharged.

Here are some legitimate ways you might be able to get all or part of your loans canceled—again, depending on the type of loan you took out. These exemptions apply for Perkins Loans only:

Teaching in a school, approved by the Department of Education, that serves low-income students or in designated teacher shortage areas. Check out other possible teacher-related loan cancellations if you took out a Perkins loan.

Serving in the U.S. military can get you a partial cancellation. If you are willing to serve in the military, there are lots of free tuition programs, so check them out before taking out any student loans.

Working full-time for a public or non-profit agency providing services to low-income, high-risk children and their families.

Working as a full-time nurse, medical technician, or law enforcement or corrections officer.

Working as a full-time staff member of a Head Start program.

Becoming a Peace Corps or VISTA volunteer.

If you have a large amount of loans that you won't be able to pay off in the foreseeable future, it might be worth working in one of these professions for a few years, if you did take out a Perkins loan.

You have the rest of your life to go back to your original career plan, which will then be student-loan free.

If none of the above professions interest you, at least try to consolidate your loans, if they are at different interest rates. A new interest rate will be applied to the amount you borrowed, which will be a weighted average, not to exceed 8.25 percent at this writing. And, if you keep a good record of making your payments on time, the lender might even offer you a discount over the course of your loan.

Some individuals defer their loans by constantly going to school. This is not always a good idea. The longer it takes to start paying down the loan, the longer it will take to pay it off. Besides, if you have to get another loan to pay the tuition, you are only going deeper into debt. If you cannot afford to make the scheduled payments on your student loan, refer to the options that you have for repayment listed in the Student Aid Borrower Services Manual published by the U. S. Department of Education. For a copy of this manual, visit my website, www.theroadtocreditrepair.com.

Big Budget Buster: Job Loss

There's nothing that wreaks havoc on your budget more than an unexpected job loss. It happens to many of us at some point in our lives, even if we have our own businesses. The trick is to be prepared for it at all times, including doing the following:

> Keeping up an emergency stash of cash. If you have a three-month cushion, hopefully you will be able to find a new job within that time. This is also where a home equity line of credit comes in handy, so it's a good idea to get one when times are good.

> Always keeping your skills updated. You will want to be the last one chosen for a layoff, so make your skills

indispensable. Take adult-education classes or any other training courses offered by your employer.

Perform your job with the utmost diligence so as to always make the employer feel as though they cannot get along without you. Give a 110-percent performance daily.

Join professional organizations or other groups where you can constantly be networking with other people in your profession. Keep a Rolodex of people to call if you ever need a job in a hurry.

Take advantage of any career counseling or outplacement services offered by your company if you are laid off. They will work with you to develop a resume, practice interview skills, and find work in your area. If your employer is not offering anything, the U.S. Department of Labor sponsors free One Stop Career Centers throughout the country. Go to www.careerone stop.org to find one closest to your area.

If you become a victim of unemployment, slash your expenses and find any kind of temporary job to pay your fixed-cost bills. Keep a cool head and remain conscious of your financial circumstances, making adjustments while weathering the storm. By doing this, you should be able to ride out the storm.

CHAPTER 19

An Invitation to Join My Inner Circle

What you did yesterday is done;
What you'll do tomorrow is unknown;
What you do today bridges the past with the future.
It is the substance within you—truth, confidence, intelligence,
spirit, and faith—that builds the bridge.
It's all in your mindset!

— DEBORAH M. DENNIS

As you can probably tell, I am a busy woman. Very busy! I'm not even above pouring concrete with my husband if we're facing a big deadline with a house we are building and he's short of help. However, I feel that with the road I have taken—from a comfortable living to the depths of financial ruin and back to wealth—I should share what I have learned with others.

I know I have made many mistakes along my own financial journey and one of the reasons I wrote this book is so you can avoid making the same mistakes. Becoming financially healthy is certainly not easy and it takes a lot of hard work and sacrifice, but the rewards are well worth it. Think of how pleasant your life will be if you can pay all of your bills, avoid debt collectors, have a good cushion in the bank for rainy days, and save for a very happy retirement. Isn't that what we all want out of life?

The trick is to find a balance so you are not overworking or overspending and to diversify your income. Remember to strive to make money while you sleep. We want time to spend with our families and we want to provide them with a good standard of living. My motivation was not so much for my own kids, but for their kids. I wanted to be sure that their futures were secure.

In addition, when my husband and I do decide to do nothing but sit on the veranda and watch the rising or the setting of the sun, I want this to happen without the stress of wondering if there will be enough money to have this freedom. Having multiple streams of income and, particularly, a stream that flows twenty-four hours a day, is the ticket to ultimate financial independence.

Strive to build the kind of life that is right for you and don't worry about keeping up with the Joneses. Trust me—the grass is not always greener on the other side of the fence. Sure, some people are born with silver spoons in their mouths and the government seems to give rich people all kinds of tax breaks. But that doesn't mean that we can't have it all, too, just because we don't fit into these categories. We can! All we have to do is make the most of our talents, be conscientious with our financial decisions, save, and prepare for the future. Just making this commitment—to ourselves, to our futures—will make our own little parts of the world be the best they can be.

Once you reach that financial plateau that makes living comfortable and you have time on your hands, your next step is to become enlightened. You are enlightened when you can think of others and, in your heart, want to share with them a part of your wealth for the betterment of their living space. To be wealthy does not necessarily mean to be rich. "Rich" is relative to your perception of it.

I urge you to give back to your community in some small way, no matter what your financial situation—whether it's financial contributions or volunteer work. While doing so, you will feel rich, very rich, as you work to improve the standard of living of those who are less fortunate than you. When you give back, you will always feel and know your blessings as you remind yourself that you could very well be in the shoes of that person you are helping.

After reading this book, you may still have many unanswered questions; perhaps I did not cover something that applies to your particular situation. Therefore, I invite you to become a part of my inner circle, where I will be offering advice as well as updates on what is going on in the world of consumer finance. Feel free to contact me at any time if I can answer a question or even just encourage you not to give up the fight. I will be your spirit guide as you start along the road to credit repair.

As we have seen, it is very easy to fall back into our old bad habits by overspending and not planning for our futures. I would be happy to give you a little pep talk now and then. Just check out my website and click on Coaching Opportunities: www.theroadtocreditrepair.com. However, promise that you will read this whole book first!

You also may be interested in what is going on in my life as my husband and I continue to expand our construction business, build residual income—and make money as we sleep. I invite you to read my weekly blog to which you are welcome to contribute on an ongoing basis. Let's all pitch in and help each other as we work to improve our financial situations. Look for me on www.theroadtocreditrepair.blogspot.com.

I invite you to go to my website and sign up for my monthly newsletter. It is free of charge. It includes photos and features success stories about people who have used my advice and techniques to recover from bankruptcy, reduce their debt, improve their credit scores, or figure out new ways to increase their weekly income. Just visit www.theroadtocreditrepair.com and register to receive the newsletter. The website also offers links to other good financial articles.

In addition, as I travel giving seminars about credit repair and building wealth through real estate across the country, you will have the opportunity to attend, meet me, and ask questions to learn more about planning your financial future, using real estate to create residual income.

I feel the need to keep writing books about my experience, so keep an eye open for future books on wealth accumulation and real estate investing. Pick up the book that tells my story— *In God We Trust: The Mindset of a Successful Real Estate Investor*. It tells the complete story of how my husband and I went from a million dollars in debt to over a million net in less than a year. I tell the complete story in this book—every detail. You can use the benefit of my victory to inspire yours.

You can never have too much knowledge about these subjects and I assure you that my story will not only inspire, but will motivate you to *just do it*. As I said, you can hear it from the experts in their ivory towers or from someone who has actually lived it, breathed it, and who genuinely cares about the success of your attempt to improve your financial situation.

Keep up your great work, never give up your fight, and do stay in touch. I am praying for you and I am confident that you will overcome your adversity and achieve your goals through financial freedom. You will be successful along your road to credit repair and debt reduction—and successful in your quest to build a positive net. I know you will!

Acknowledgements

First and foremost, I thank God for the favor of His grace which includes my mother, my family, my friends, and my pastor. Thank you, my Father in Heaven, for all of your blessings and the granting of the wisdom that I pray for daily.

During the course of writing this book, I hit highs and lows. Because of some incredibly special people that God has placed in my life, this book personifies a dream. I have so many people to thank for the inspiration to write this book. I would be remiss if I did not start with my husband, W. T. Dennis, Jr., who supported me, every step of the way, inevitably taking my visions and turning them into reality, time after time. Not only is he the wind beneath my wings, he is literally the reason for the best that comes out of me. Thank you, Husband, for nearly thirty-five years of bliss.

Thank you to my grandbabies, Kynidi and Frederick Jackson, whose future motivates me to rise in the morning and "just get to it" so their future can be favorable for the accomplishment of greatness.

To my girls, Nikisha "Kish" Jackson and Chevella "Joy" Dennis, my heart and soul; I thank you for your love and the confidence that you inspire within me twenty-four hours of each and every day and I am extremely proud of the women you both have turned out to be.

Thank you to my mother, Thyra Reddix Morris and my aunt, Fannie Reddix Irvin, my biggest fans, and for being my spirit guides for all that I do.

Thank you to my sister, Clarencetta Irvin Cosey, for taking up the slack with our elders, so I can pursue my vision knowing that my mother and my aunt have someone that I trust caring and watching out for them.

Thanks so very much, David Smith and Charlie Henderson, our lenders who provided the financing so that we could hold on to the dream of the Enchanted Villas, when we needed traditional lending the most. We could not have won without your support.

Thanks, Timothy Plummer, for providing that first opportunity to build. It was the start of a promising career and we owe it all to you. We will always be grateful for that opportunity and your confidence in us.

Thank you to my brother in Christ, Henry Adley, my cousin, Claudette Reddix Brown, and her daughter, Latawnya Brown Johnson, my sister in Christ, Jessie Gardner King, and our friends indeed, Willie and Marion Erby, whose financial and spiritual support are the reasons that the dream of the Enchanted Villas Subdivision materialized—without which, I would not have had anything to base this book.

Thank you, Chris Shaw, for having your confidence in our ability to be a successful bank customer. Your bank loans put us on the road to recovery.

Thanks, Mike Wells, for funding our dream to make money as we sleep. You and Chris are the best in banking.

Thanks my godchild, Lisa Cosey Hunt; your Nanny is proud of your drive and ability and I thank you for your admiration for what I do, the way I do it.

Thank you to my aunt, Frances Pierce Reddix, my surrogate mother, for your constant encouragement and enthusiasm for all that I do.

Thank you, my cousin and sister at heart, Dr. Ollibeth Reddix Mosby, for our conversations and your vision of how high I can soar. Thank you to my godparents, Dr. Herman and Patricia Yvonne Dupree Walker, and my cousin and his wife, Dr. James "Andrew" and Gwendolyn Dupree, for filling my head with the confidence that "yes, I can."

Thank you my little cousin, Sandra O. J. Nesbitt, for your abilities as a professional graphic designer and the generous manner in which you helped me critique the cover for this book.

Thanks to my architect, George Hicks: I will always be grateful for your role in the development of the Enchanted Villas and for each time that you have taken our vision and turned it into a blueprint. God could not have given us a better mentor. Thanks to your wife, Dotty, for being by your side and ours, I will never forget her tip to the newspaper.

Thanks Delwyn Morton for your wisdom and support, I am eternally grateful for all of the doors of opportunity that opened as a result of your friendship and generosity.

Thank you to my family—brother, sisters, nieces, nephews, and cousins—who comprise the Reddix clan of quality producing individuals for carrying on the legacy gifted by Papa Reddix. Your awesome achievements keep me on my toes, reaching higher and higher.

Thank you to my brother in Christ, Robert "Bob" Allen, for encouraging me to bring the book inside of me to print. Thank you to my agents, Bob Allen and Richard Paul Evans, for WriteWise and an entire team of professionals and supporters that expeditiously bailed me out of a jamb. Thank you, specifically, to Karen Christoffersen for being the greatest producer and friend that anyone can be blessed to have while writing a book. You will never know the depth of my gratitude for your patience, quick thinking, and actions.

Thank you to my co-hosts on the Hour of Power with a View radio broadcast, my long time friend and my sister at heart, Dr. Patricia Russell-Harrison, and Kevin Brown, for partnering with me to disseminate wealth building strategies all over the world.

Thank you to Dr. Lauretta Byars, Vice-president of Institutional Relations at Prairie View A & M University and all of the instructors, administrators, faculty, and staff at the Prairie View A & M University, for keeping a watchful eye on my baby girl, Joy; the comfort of knowing that she was in good hands freed me to concentrate on this book.

Thanks to my dearest friends, Mary Helen Ponder and Tyrone Holly, for just being there to pitch in wherever and whenever, making my vision and mission on so many occasions, yours.

Thank you, Father Timothy Gollob, for instilling in me, through your teaching, the spiritual confidence that Jesus Christ lives in my heart.

Thanks to you my Holy Cross brothers and sisters in Christ for embracing me as your sister in Christ: the Fergusons, the Vaults, Lari Newman-Williams, the Voices of Love Choir, the Inspirational Friends, the Altar Society, and many, many more that space limits acknowledging.

A special thanks to the members of The Ultimate Group for your friendship that spans more than twenty years and your constant encouragement.

Thanks to you, all of the homeowners of the Enchanted Villas Subdivision, for buying into our vision of building a community of elegance in the southern sector of Dallas. Without your support, Enchanted Villas would have been a builder's nightmare. Thank you, Willis Johnson, for using your show to give the Enchanted Villas much needed exposure during the calm after the storm. It was a mighty generous thing you did, and we will always be grateful. Thank you, Penny and Robert Pitre, for sharing your ranch to host our victory party, and for bringing so many valuable people into our business and personal lives. Thanks, Reginald Gates, for being the best leader that a community chamber of commerce can have, and for supporting the many times I've had to use you to support and further my causes. Thank you, Milton and Cotille Pettit (Jokaes Bookstore), for your many years of support and friendship.

There are so many other people of my extended family and among my friends that I need to thank in print, whose footprint and fingerprints have been an inspiration for me to do what I believe I have an obligation to do. Just know that your presence in my life is lovingly and indelibly etched in my heart and I thank you from the very bottom of my soul to the tip of my being for just existing in my life, for caring for my family, my vision, and my many causes. Be Blessed All!

- Deborah M. Dennis

302

About the Author

Stepping off of the corporate train to become an entrepreneurs, Deborah M. Dennis is a respected real estate developer, home builder, real estate investor and philanthropist who facilitates dreams of home ownership for many people in Texas. She has been honored by the community Chamber of Commerce in Dallas for her success as an entrepreneur, cited in the Dallas Morning News and community newspapers for her work in community development, and inducted into the Business and Professional Women's Hall of Fame. Holding a bachelor's and a master's degree in Computer Science from Texas A & M University at Commerce, Deborah used her skills as a computer scientist to develop a strategy for improving credit scores and reducing debt. Working to build wealth is the premise for the world-wide radio broadcast that she hosts: *The Hour of Power with a View.* Through this Internet broadcast coupled with her seminars and retreats, she accomplishes her mission to encourage the elimination of debt and the building of wealth. Working with college students on how to become entrepreneurs, she has in her plans a book to promote success strategies for post-graduate collegiates. Her goal is to bring many books in the future on the subject of building wealth, specifically as a real estate investor. Currently, she resides in Dallas, Texas with her husband, two kids, and two grandchildren.